BABY SLEEP AND ANGER MANAGEMENT FOR TIRED PARENTS

2-in-1 Book

How to Improve Your Emotional Self-Control and Manage Your Anger + How to Help Your Baby to Sleep Through the Night

BABY SLEEP: NO-CRY BABY SOLUTION FOR TIRED PARENTS

Stress Free Guide With All Helpful Tips And Information That You Need To Help Your Baby To Sleep Through The Night

Baby Sleep

Table of Contents

Introduction 7

Chapter 1 - The Basics of Baby Sleep 11

   Baby Sleep Cycles By Age 11

   How Do Sleep Cycles Differ By Age? 14

   5 Fascinating Facts About Your Baby's Sleep 17

   Important Precautions To Keep Your Baby Safe As They Sleep . 19

   What About Co-sleeping? 21

   What About You? How To Manage On Broken Sleep 22

Chapter 2 - Getting Organized 26

   Everything You Need for Your Baby's Sleeping Area 26

   Where Should Your Baby Sleep? 28

   Sleep Associations: What They Are & How They Can Help 29

   What is a Sleep Log? 35

Chapter 3 - Baby Sleep Problems 37

   8 Common Baby Sleep Problems by Age & How to Manage Them
.... 37

   Fixing Less Common Reasons for Poor Sleep 41

   What Your Baby's Sleep Habits Mean 44

Chapter 4 - Preparing for Sleep Training 47

   Hard Truths about Sleep Training that All Parents Must Know ... 48

   Is Your Baby Ready for Sleep Training? 52

   How to Choose the Right Sleep Training Method for Your Baby 55

Chapter 5 - Sleep Training Success 57

   4 Transformative Sleep Training Methods 57

   Sleep Training in More Detail: Here's How 60

How to Make Sure Your Baby Sleeps Through the Night........... 63
Why Sleep Training Fails & What to Do 64

Chapter 6 - It's Naptime! 67
Strategies for a Successful Naptime 68
What if Your Baby Won't Nap? 70

Chapter 7 - No Problem Too Big 73
Understanding Sleep Regressions by Age 73
How to Deal With Sleep Regressions 76
6 Must-Know Sleep Strategies for Single Parents 78
Two Babies, Many Solutions 81

Chapter 8 - Completing Your No-Cry Toolkit 85
How to Soothe a Crying Baby 85
Baby Crying Patterns by Age 87
5 Effective Remedies for Colic 88
Helping a Sick Baby Get Restful Sleep 91

Conclusion 95

Introduction

Lack of sleep is one of the things many parents find most unbearable when they come home with a new baby. And for a certain amount of time, it's simply part and parcel of being a new parent. But there are things you can do to make your baby sleep better, and this book will give you all the information you need to enjoy more peaceful nights with your baby or toddler.

By the end of it, you should feel ready to make the right choices for your family about sleep training, along with setting up a daily routine, handling naps and illness, and dealing with a crying baby. I have tried here to distil both everything I have learned from raising two babies, and everything that the parenting experts know about babies, toddlers and sleep.

Sleep training isn't always easy, and it can lead to a few upset nights. A crying baby is hard for any parent, and if you've picked up this book because you have tried and failed to get your baby to sleep, you have my sympathy. Learning to fall asleep, and stay asleep is something that comes more naturally to some babies. But for others, unfortunately, it takes time and effort on the part of often exhausted parents to support their baby to sleep deeply and wake up refreshed and happy.

Add in curveballs such as colic and common childhood illnesses, plus parents dealing with more than one baby, or single parenthood, and it's no wonder new parents are struggling.

If this is you, you're no doubt exhausted and wondering what to do next – should you try sleep training, controlled crying, or some other technique you haven't read about yet? Are you doing something wrong? Is there something wrong with your baby? What is the secret of those mothers who have such 'good' babies; those who sleep through the night without complaint?

Rest assured, it is completely normal to ask all of these questions throughout your parenting journey. But please know that sleep problems are also totally normal with babies and toddlers, and over time things will improve. Babies simply need to adjust to the world they've arrived in, and some find this easier than others. This doesn't make them 'good' or 'bad' babies – it just makes each of them unique! Sleep problems in the early years are simply part of being a parent, and don't mean you are doing anything wrong. Sometimes, working around the poor sleep and finding ways to cope is your best option, and I will show you how to do that in the chapters to follow, along with safe and gentle sleep training options.

If you are due to have your first baby soon and want to get ahead with your parenting skills, this book will also be very useful and make those early days a little easier.

The best training is on-the-job, and as a mother who has raised two babies, I have been through the early, sleep-deprived days of living with a new baby, and know what worked for me. It may not be exactly what works for your baby – that is for you to discover. What is easy for one baby may not be easy at all for another, which is why it can be frustrating to receive so many different pieces of advice from well-meaning outsiders who don't know your baby as well as you do. Your instincts about what your baby needs are always worth listening to. Let them guide you as you find your way, and remember, even if people sound like they know so much more than you, everyone who parents is mostly winging it.

I don't try to offer my readers a perfect one-size-fits-all solution (which, when it comes to parenting, doesn't exist anyway). What I offer to you instead is a range of strategies to try, all based on sound research and the latest findings around baby sleep. All are based on both looking after my own babies and doing my own extensive research and reading around baby sleep. As someone who looks back on those sleep-deprived early days with mixed feelings, I always think of things I could have done better. Personally, with my first baby, I let the broken nights go on for far too long. With my second, I was more confident about taking charge, and he was a better sleeper from an earlier age.

Read on to discover all of the different things you can try to get your baby to sleep better. When you try these approaches, you can look forward to a less fretful and exhausted baby who will be far more engaged and happy in his or her waking hours. The other, very important, benefit will be for you – with more sleep and less time trying to get your baby to sleep, you'll feel so much better, have more energy and be able to get on with the business of living alongside your baby.

As with anything to do with your baby, it's always worth getting an expert opinion if there's anything that's bothering you. Help is out there, and you only have to ask. But for many parents, it's simply a matter of knowing what to expect and how you can guide your baby in the right direction.

I will also cover in detail all of the things you need to think about in relation to safe sleep – the equipment you need, where your baby should sleep, and how to avoid any accidents. We'll cover strange sleeping habits, how to keep a sleep log and how to carry out sleep training, should you feel it's what you need for your own and your family's well being. Nap times, sleep regression, and getting your baby to sleep well when she is sick are other areas you may find helpful at particular times on your journey. And we'll look at sleep issues for single parents, as well as those looking after more than one baby.

What I offer are not clear solutions, but a framework and guidelines for you to try, to see what works for you. When it comes to babies and toddlers, this is the only sane approach! Rest assured that by establishing routines and a gentle timetable around sleep, as well as some consistency, you will be well on your way to better nights.

So settle back, and work through this book in your own time, taking note of what works for your baby, leaving behind what doesn't, and may trying things a little further on down the track – sometimes your baby just needs a little more time.

I promise that by the end of it, you'll have many new ideas to work with, and will be starting to see the light at the end of the tunnel. What I don't want you to do is fall into despair about your baby's sleep – these precious months when your baby is small will pass quickly, and ideally there should be many moments of joy for you, too.

Let me assure you again that there are many ways in which you can help your baby become a better, longer sleeper. Please know that when this happens, your daily life together will become so much easier. It's also worth remembering that not all problems can be solved by you, but by the passing of time – your baby will grow up a little, learn new skills, and suddenly what was bothering you about their sleep has simply stopped happening. This is one of the most amazing things about parenting – watching as your child grows up, develops, learns new skills and becomes their own person. Each stage brings its own rewards along with the questions.

As well as helping your baby adjust to the world, you also have to take charge constantly as a parent, always noting what works for your particular baby. Sleep is one of the key areas you will need to focus on and feel confident about as you start your new life with your baby. And as a parent, acting with consistency and confidence is often the key to success.

Here is a guide to help you do just that.

Chapter 1 - The Basics of Baby Sleep

In this section, we'll touch on baby sleep cycles by age, so you can understand your baby's sleeping habits better. Babies change so quickly at this stage of life as their brains and bodies grow rapidly. Having a basic understanding of what to expect from your baby's sleep at each stage, and what you'll need to wait a little longer for, can be both helpful and reassuring to new parents.

Like everything else they have to master, babies need to **learn** how to sleep at night and stay awake during the day – it isn't something they can do from day one. It's also helpful to know that the wakefulness and unsettled sleep of a tiny newborn is partly a survival mechanism to keep them from falling too deeply asleep when they need to feed regularly and their lungs are still so new. Better sleep does come with time, and this is something all parents need to accept to some extent. What you can do, though, is understand what to expect at each stage, and in later chapters we'll look at how to nudge your baby in the direction of good sleep habits.

In this chapter we'll also give you five fascinating facts about your baby's sleep. And finally, we'll cover the all-important precautions you can take when setting up your baby's sleeping area to keep him or her safe during naps and night time sleeping.

Ready? Let's get started.

Baby Sleep Cycles By Age

Baby Sleep

As a rough guide to work with, here's how much sleep babies and toddlers will need over a 24-hour period, varying between naps and longer sleeps at night.

Newborns: 16 hours, though it can be as little as eight and as much as 18

Three-month-old babies: around 15 hours

Two years plus: around 12 hours

Of course, as with everything, these times can vary between individual babies, and you'll quickly gain a sense of your own baby's sleep patterns. You'll also soon learn to value their sleep and do whatever you can to protect it, as it results in a much happier, more contented baby in their waking hours. And not only will a well-rested baby be more enjoyable and easy to be around, regular, deep sleep is essential for their growth and development.

One of the biggest shocks I received when I brought my first baby home from the hospital was when I tried to put him to bed on that first, exhausted night. *That was all pretty intense*, I thought to myself, *but at least now we can all have a good night's sleep and see where we are in the morning.*

For some reason, I simply assumed that because we were home, life would return to normal. He would understand that it was late and we were going to sleep now, right?

Of course, it didn't work out that way. The minute I turned off the light, my baby was wide awake and screaming for two hours solid as I tried to feed him, soothe him, comfort him – and get him back to sleep. Many unsettled nights followed, and it took me a while to get that full night's sleep I was expecting, but eventually, sleep and sanity returned. Sorting out feeding problems helped a lot, but much of it was due to him being so new to the world and unsettled by everything and everyone around him.

What I also soon realised from talking to my midwives and my own research was that newborns have no sense of night or day. To some extent, their sleep patterns are governed by their mother when they are in the womb, and the rise and fall of her own activity and hormone levels. But once they are born, their mother's movements no longer dictate their sleeping and waking times, and they need to establish their own sleep habits in time with the outside world.

You may notice that your baby seems particularly alert at night, which is totally normal for newborns. This will generally start to get better at around six weeks old, which is when the intensity of the newborn phase – the screaming, colicky hours and the unsettled behaviour – will often start to ease a little generally. It can be helpful to think of the first three months as a 'fourth trimester' when your baby is still adjusting to life outside the womb, and keep your environment as peaceful as you can, particularly if you have an unsettled, nervous baby (if you do, you'll know what this means.)

Having said all that, you may also wonder if there are there any ways of speeding up this process of getting newborns into a normal day-night sleep cycle? Yes! There's lots you can do. Playing with your baby and taking him outside in the daytime, and creating a quiet, dim, even boring, environment at night, will help him to learn that night is for sleeping. As adults, our sleep is governed by circadian rhythms – we feel alert during the hours of daylight, especially if we go outside and expose ourselves to natural light soon after waking, and at night time, when the lights begin to dim, our bodies produce melatonin, which readies us for sleep.

Your baby will soon do the same, but in the meantime, it's best to simply allow for the broken sleep, let other people take care of you, don't try and do too much or worry about "getting into a routine." For now, as much as you can, simply enjoy the precious newborn bubble. You can and will sleep later, I promise!

How Do Sleep Cycles Differ By Age?

Adult sleep cycles consist of deep 'soundless' sleep and REM or active sleep, which is also the dreaming phase of sleep and essential for healthy brain function, as it's when your brain essentially puts all its files in order. During REM sleep, the body is temporarily paralysed, but brain activity is noticeable, with irregular breathing and eye movements. An adult sleep cycle will last about 90 minutes, and at the end of it we either wake up or start a new cycle. Baby's sleep cycles are slightly different, and it helps to be aware of this.

Newborns (birth to three months)

A newborn will cycle between quiet and active sleep, and each cycle is shorter than an adult sleep cycle at about an hour long, up until around nine months of age. Unlike adults, babies will **begin** with active sleep, which is similar to REM in adults, and are more likely to wake up in this stage, particularly if they jerk and startle themselves. Around half of their sleep is spent in 'active sleep', compared to only 20 per cent for adults. While babies are asleep, their movements during this sleep may mean that the adult assumes they are waking up. But often, if they are left alone at this point, they will continue to sleep. This need to be 'held together' to fall into a deep sleep is why many babies respond well to firm swaddling, up until the age of about two months.

Around halfway through the sleep cycle, the baby will settle into a quiet sleep, with slower breathing, stillness and no eyelid fluttering. This is the end of the sleep cycle, after which the baby will either awaken, or begin a new cycle of active sleep. You will soon start to recognise the quiet sleep, which is less unsettled. However, very small babies tend not to have periods of long, deep sleep as older babies do.

By three months of age, rather than starting in REM or active sleep, babies will start a sleep cycle in deep sleep, like adults, which can make it easier for them to fall and stay asleep.

You'll find that once your baby starts onto solid food, around six months, their sleep will improve even more, and once they start moving independently they will tire themselves out more and sleep even better.

Newborns will tend to sleep off and on throughout the day, and while you can't control this completely, you can work around it and gently guide them towards sleeping at night and being awake during the day, with a couple of naps in between.

Newborns are also often quite light sleepers and will spend about half their time in active, not deep sleep. Because they are so small, their bellies can't hold much food so they will wake regularly to feed – as they grow, they will wake less often and will eventually 'sleep through' until (early) morning.

You'll also notice that a "good sleeper" won't necessarily stay that way. Newborns may start off sleeping very deeply and regularly, but at around three weeks they will start to become less settled — sleeping less and crying more, often for no apparent reason. Around this time you may see one longer sleep of up to five or six hours, a couple of three hour sleeps, several two hour sleeps and five or six hours of drowsing, crying, and catnapping. No wonder parents of newborns are exhausted from all that broken sleep!

Infants (three to 11 months)

Baby Sleep

By three months, your baby may have settled into a regular routine, with a morning and afternoon sleep and sometimes an extra one, too. The morning sleep tends to be quite long, with one or two afternoon naps to follow before bedtime.

You can expect your baby to sleep for around 14-15 hours a day, with some babies sleeping for up to eight hours at night.

The active sleep phase is reduced, and they will start to sleep more deeply. You can expect them to wake at least once at night, with some babies waking every three hours for a feed.

At around six months, the total amount of sleep a baby has per 24 hour cycle will reduce to about 13 hours a day in total. The naps will also reduce – many babies drop the morning nap first (a sad day, but it also means you can go out more easily in the mornings!), but continue to have one or two afternoon sleeps. However, many children will continue having an after-lunch nap well into toddlerhood.

At around six months of age, babies will also begin to move towards a more typical sleep cycle, with longer cycles and less time in active sleep. Gradually, over time, they will build up to sleeping for a solid eight to 12 hours of uninterrupted sleep.

Babies at this age will also usually sleep better at night, though some may wake up and need to be settled back to sleep, often with a feed. Separation anxiety, which appears at this age, can also cause some babies to feel more clingy and wake in the night for reassurance, particularly if they have been separated from you during the day.

Establishing daytime and bedtime routines and creating a flexible structure can help your baby to get to sleep at night. We will cover all of this in detail in the chapters that follow.

Toddlers (12 to 36 months)

Around 12 months, your baby will start to move into toddlerhood. With this increased maturity, and more movement and activity in their daily life, they will be sleeping better at night and only wake up once or perhaps twice at night.

By the time they are around two, they will need approximately 12 hours' sleep over a 24-hour period, although they may have longer sleeps during growth spurts and developmental leaps – if this happens, work around it, as they really do need as much sleep as they can get at this age, when their brains are growing so quickly. We will cover the sleep regression that sometimes comes with growth spurts in later chapters. Sometimes, I would notice my toddler having an especially long, deep sleep, and waking up with a new skill that I hadn't seen before – it was as if the extra sleep had actually been an intense training session for a developmental leap.

5 Fascinating Facts About Your Baby's Sleep

1. The more they sleep, the more they sleep

An overtired, fretful baby can find it difficult to get to sleep, then find it hard to enjoy being awake, creating a cycle of bad sleeping. But good sleep creates more of the same. So keeping a baby awake when they are tired, to try and make them sleep better at night, will actually have the opposite effect. It seems counterintuitive, but a wired, overtired baby will find it harder to get to sleep than one who is put to bed earlier. Prioritising your baby's daytime sleep and getting into a regular routine is the best way of working towards better nights, and this is what we will focus on throughout this book.

2. Morning light promotes good sleep

Taking in natural light in the daytime, and creating a dimly lit environment at night, will stimulate the production of melatonin, a hormone that promotes sleep. This works for adults as well as babies – going outside and getting some natural light on your face soon after you wake up can be helpful if you suffer from insomnia as it 'sets' your body clock. Be sure to get outside with your baby – for a walk around the park, to the shops, or just out in your back garden – every day, so that they start to set their body clocks as quickly as possible. As we'll cover in later chapters, the variety and stimulation babies get from being outside is also an essential and easy aid to encourage better sleeping at night.

3. Babies take longer to reach a deep sleep – around 20 minutes.

Because babies start off in active, not deep sleep, they can move and grimace a lot in their sleep. So even if your baby seems unsettled, leaving them in peace will often result in them reaching deep sleep eventually. If you can, try to resist rushing in to soothe or pick them up when they first fall down – they may seem upset, but in fact they are busy falling asleep, or very close to it. If you find this difficult, force yourself to go and have a five-minute shower. You won't be able to hear any crying, you'll get five minutes to yourself, and you may just come out and find that your baby has fallen asleep in your absence.

4. Night waking are essential to their survival.

While it can be frustrating being woken through the night, your baby needs to wake up to fill their tiny belly. Once they are a little bigger, their sleep cycles will lengthen and you won't have such broken nights. They also may wake up suddenly due to a startle reflex and getting them back to sleep can be difficult. As mentioned earlier, some parents find that swaddling their baby in a soft blanket or sheet can hold them still and help them settle and stay asleep for longer. Swaddling is easy and often helps with broken sleep – look online for videos of how to swaddle a baby.

5. Babies learn as they sleep.

During REM sleep, research shows that blood flow to the baby's brain increases, as their brains work hard to integrate all the new information they have been given that day. Sleep is essential to brain development, so the more you can learn about sleep techniques and help your baby to achieve them, the better. During REM sleep you may notice your baby twitch, breath irregularly and move their eyes. They stay in REM sleep for about half of each cycle, which may be because at this age, they have so much learning to do. For this reason, too, you should avoid waking a sleeping baby as much as possible (as if you would!).

Important Precautions To Keep Your Baby Safe As They Sleep

To keep your baby safe as they sleep, here are some essential guidelines to follow. We will cover some of the points in more detail in the following chapters.

- Always put babies to sleep on their backs, both at night and when they have daytime naps. Once they are a little older, they may find their own position as they move around throughout the night, but always put them to bed on their back.

- Sleeping should be done only on a firm surface, such as a mattress in a safety-approved crib or bassinet. Avoid soft fluffy blankets or cushions.

Baby Sleep

- It's recommended that you share a room with your baby for the first six months. A cot attached to your bed, with an open side that can be dropped down for feeds, is a solution that will ensure everyone gets enough sleep. Babies often sleep better if they know their parent is in the room, although once you attempt sleep training you will need to move your baby (or yourself) into another room, at least temporarily – more on this later.

- Use a fitted sheet and keep all soft objects, toys, padding and pillows away from the sleeping area. A zip-up sleeping bag with a fitted neck and armholes is a safe option for sleep as it can't cover the baby's face. These sleeping bags come in different thicknesses so you can choose the right one for your climate and time of year. They also serve as a useful sleep cue, telling your baby it's time to go to bed – again, more on sleep cues later.

- Never smoke around your baby, or allow other people to smoke in areas where your baby spends time. If someone has been smoking, they shouldn't hold a small baby. Smoking is associated with an increased risk of SIDS, so keep your environment completely smoke-free, and avoid it when you are out, too, especially if your baby was sick or premature at birth.

- Never fall asleep with your baby on a sofa or other area apart from the safe sleeping area. If you want to sleep close to your baby, set up an open cot next to you bed so the baby is close but safely out of the way. Planning co-sleeping like this is far safer than accidental co-sleeping, particularly when everyone is exhausted and can fall asleep very deeply.

- Never sleep near your baby if you have been drinking alcohol or are otherwise under the influence of drugs, or particularly exhausted. And never allow others who are under the influence of drugs or alcohol to fall asleep near your baby either. Pets should not share a sleeping area with babies, either.

- Keep an eye on the temperature of the room and ensure that it remains comfortable – not too hot or too cold. Keep your baby's head uncovered, and dress them in the same amount of clothing you would wear to bed. Overheated babies are at an increased risk of SIDS.

- Ensure everyone looking after the baby, or living in the house, is aware of safe sleeping practices, too. And finally, babies should never be left alone to sleep in cars, or in car seats, or unsupervised in prams.

What About Co-sleeping?

Some parents choose to co-sleep with their babies, and find that it works very well. Others don't choose to co-sleep but find instead that it chooses them, as their baby will not settle anywhere else but close to them at night. If you do choose to co-sleep, ensure that you are doing so safely. Sharing a bed is not safe if the baby is sharing a bed with a smoker, or if there are adult blankets that may cover the baby, or if the parent is drunk, drugged, obese or very tired.

If you do choose to co-sleep, ensure that your mattress is very firm, and that the baby cannot fall off the bed (a mattress on the floor is the safest option.) Put the baby on one side of the bed, not between two adults, dressed in a sleeping bag, not covered in adult blankets, and ensure that everyone knows the baby is in the bed.

You should also be aware that the risk of Sudden Infant Death while co-sleeping is most common in the first eleven weeks. Personally, at this age, I had my babies in a cot next to my bed, with one side removed, so there was no chance of me rolling onto them, but they were close by. Once they were older, they sometimes ended up next to me in bed, but for the most part they were in their own safe space. As with everything, it's always worth talking to your doctor and child health nurse before making a decision that works for you and your family. As mentioned earlier, accidental or unplanned co-sleeping, when you fall asleep with your baby unintentionally, is more dangerous than planned co-sleeping.

So now you know the basics of baby sleep from birth to toddlerhood, and know what you can expect in terms of sleep quality and length at each age. You also know how to set up a safe sleeping area for your baby. Let's move on to ways you can encourage deep, refreshing sleep for your baby so that he or she thrives and is happier in the daytime. But first, let's look at how to manage as a new parent on broken sleep.

What About You? How To Manage On Broken Sleep

Now that we've established that you won't be getting a full eight hours' sleep a night for some time, let's have a quick look at how you can help yourself through these early days. This time will pass, and you will sleep again, but it's important to go easy on yourself and not feel like you have to be your normal, well-rested self. Personally, I found the broken sleep and tiredness to be the hardest part of being a new parent. I couldn't hold proper conversations, I felt flat and exhausted a lot of the time, and I couldn't seem to think clearly or plan for the future. In retrospect, I wish I'd gone a bit easier on myself – napped more, gone to bed earlier, and not worried so much about the future and "getting everything under control." If you find you are really struggling, always seek help early from your doctor, in particular if you find you can't sleep yourself, even at night time.

Some baby experts refer to the first three months after the baby's birth as a Fourth Trimester. By this, they mean it's a time when you are still very much in the pregnancy and birth bubble, and should be resting and nesting much as you did towards the end of your pregnancy.

It's also a time when your baby is adjusting to life outside the womb, and you're getting to know your new baby and learning to be his parent and read his signals. Let's now look at some ways to make what can be a rough and intense time easier for you. This, in turn, will make it easier for your baby.

Tips to help you get through the early days on broken sleep.

- Mark your calendar for three months after the birth, and allow yourself, in that time, to take it easy, rest and focus on simply feeding your baby and yourself, and getting as much sleep as you can. Of course you won't be able to do this all the time. And you may feel thrilled that your pregnancy is over and ready to be out and about much sooner, especially if your baby turns out to be a good sleeper. But at least allow yourself to take it a bit easier in that first intense newborn stage – particularly if you don't have a great deal of family support around you, as many of us don't.

- Prepare ahead with some frozen meals, and perhaps get a regular online shopping order set up. Hire a cleaner, if your budget allows, or some extra help around the house, such as a post-natal nurse or night nurse. Allow others to help if they offer, with offers of food or just holding the baby so you can get a rest or a shower.

- Limit your obligations and don't feel bad for saying no to visitors, particularly those demanding ones who expect to be waited on while they hold the baby. It's natural for everyone around you to be excited about a new baby, and want to spend as much time as possible cuddling and holding the new

Baby Sleep

addition. But keep visits short if you don't feel up to it, and if your baby doesn't like being handed around for hours (many find it stressful and it can lead to an unsettled night) then simply take your baby and retreat to your bedroom. There is plenty of time for everyone to get to know your baby in the months and years ahead, and you have to prioritise your own well-being, and that of your newborn, at this special time.

- Sleep when the baby sleeps. Hard to do, when it feels like the only time you have 'off', but try not to stay awake if you could be sleeping, whenever possible. In the evenings, having a warm bath and some skin-to-skin with your baby and then an hour or two of sleep. This will make a big difference to how you feel the next morning. Especially if it ends up being an unsettled night!

- Agree on a timetable with your partner about who does night time wake ups. If you fall asleep early, perhaps your partner can do the first wake-up feed of the night, so you will get a good four or five hours of sleep before the next one – express a bottle of milk if you are breastfeeding, or have him wake and bring the baby to you, then settle him outside of the bedroom so you can fall straight back to sleep. Sharing the broken sleep means that the burden isn't just on one person.

- Prioritise eating well. When you are exhausted it can be easy to fall into the habit of existing on toast and coffee. But you will need nutritious food to recover from the birth, and to keep your energy levels high. Have some cut-up fruit and vegetables close to hand, enjoy soup, yogurt, salad and other easy meals. Drink lots of water, and try and get some protein and healthy carbohydrates into your diet, too. Keep taking your pre-natal vitamins as you rest and recover from the birth, and don't drink too much coffee, as it can interfere with your sleep.

- Finally, remember that time spent with your baby is the most important thing right now, as she settles into the world and your bond grows. Give yourself lots of time to settle her. Ask visitors to make their own drinks rather than waiting on them hand and foot. And put your feet up as much as you can. You've just been through a huge physical and emotional life change, and you need to treat yourself accordingly!

Chapter 2 - Getting Organized

We now know what babies and toddlers should be doing when it comes to sleep. We know that newborns are naturally unsettled, and that there are things we can do to help them along as they learn how to sleep properly, such as getting some natural light in the daytime. And we know how to set up a safe sleeping area for the baby.

What we also need to understand is that there's no magic trick to create a perfect sleeper – sometimes you just get lucky, other times you have a fretful baby who struggles to fall and stay asleep. What you can do is educate yourself about how to encourage good sleep.

In this chapter we'll build on this knowledge and dive into how we can establish the right environment for good sleep. We'll learn about sleep associations, and how they can help your baby to get ready to drift off. And we'll also look at creating a sleep log, which can help you develop a better understanding of how your baby's sleep is changing over time. This can be helpful both for your own peace-of-mind, and also to show your GP or child health nurse, should you decide to seek further help with your baby's sleeping habits.

Everything You Need for Your Baby's Sleeping Area

- Sheets: Around six cot or bassinet sheets is perfect, and you can also use folded single-bed sheets if you need to. You can also put a pillowcase over a small mattress when your baby is very little.
- A mattress protector to put over the mattress will protect it from leaking bottles and nappies. Or use a blanket or a towel underneath the sheet.
- A mosquito net may be helpful in the warmer months, if you live in a mosquito-prone area. There is nothing worse than waking up to a miserable baby covered in mosquito bites.

Baby Sleep

- A cot or bassinet. A small bassinet is great for the first few months, but you can also put your baby in a cot from the start. Ideally you want something that's easy to move, and that allows you to access your baby easily, for example during night feeds and if you need to pat your baby to sleep.

Some cots come with two levels, so you can raise them when the baby is small then lower them once your baby is old enough to climb out of the cot.

When choosing a cot, look for smooth, rounded edges and no extra decorations such as beads, which can be hazardous. The cot should have high sides so your baby can't fall out once they are a bit older (ie two feet from the base of the mattress to the top of the cot sides). If it has drop-sides, they need to be childproof and work smoothly, and the mattress should fit the cot well. Your cot also needs to have no more than two to three inches between bars, so your baby can't fit his or her head through.

If you are buying a second-hand or vintage cot, be aware that old paint may contain lead. You'll need to strip or repaint the cot, if this is the case. Also ensure that any decorations on an old cot can't be pulled off, and that the cot is strong and sturdy.

- Babies tend to settle and sleep better on a dense, firm mattress, so look for these when you are shopping around. A good-quality clean, firm, second-hand mattress is fine – just leave it in the sun for a day or two to air it out.

- Cot bumpers (a soft piece of padded fabric that surrounds the inside of the cot) are no longer recommended by baby safety experts, as they can restrict air flow to the cot and also pose risks of suffocation or strangulation, should they come loose. There should be absolutely no extra fabric, pillows or soft toys

Baby Sleep

around a sleeping baby. Children do not need pillows until they move into a toddler bed.

Do you need any additional safety products?

There is no substitute for planning your baby's sleeping environment and following the latest safety guidelines, remaining vigilant and using your common sense and instincts when it comes to keeping your baby safe while sleeping.

Having said that, a night light can be very helpful to cope with night feeds, and so you can move around without waking the baby too much. It can also be a comfort to your baby once they are older and wake in the middle of the night.

A sound monitor can be used if your baby's nap area is a long way away from your living room for day time naps. If your baby sleeps in your room for the first six month, you won't need it for night time – you'll hear him! However, sleep monitors don't monitor breathing, so can't be considered a safety device, and one downside is that they can be disruptive, as you will hear every noise your baby makes while sleeping.

Breathing monitors may be given to small or unwell babies, but are not generally used for all babies. They have an alarm that goes off if the baby stops breathing, but can also give frequent false alarms. I always recommend that all parents should know how to do heart-lung resuscitation, though, so you know what to do in an emergency.

Where Should Your Baby Sleep?

Ideally, for the first six months, your baby should sleep in your room for safety reasons. If, after this point, you decide you would like the baby in a separate room, the risk of SIDS (Sudden Infant Death Syndrome) drops, but it is still safer to have the baby in your room for the first six months, and as long as you like into the future. Refer to the first chapter for information about co-sleeping safely, or consider having a cot next to your bed so you can hear and reach your baby easily.

Sleep Associations: What They Are & How They Can Help

Sleep associations are essentially signals that make your baby feel sleepy. As adults, we develop them too – reading in bed before sleep, a warm bath, a particular time each night that we head for bed, and our pre-bed rituals such as brushing our teeth and putting on our pyjamas.

Setting up sleep associations for babies is much the same thing, and as your baby grows and you settle into living with him or her, you'll find a routine around sleep will help you to organise your days better and enjoy a well-rested, happy baby.

Read on for some ways you can create sleep associations and start to establish a routine with your baby.

Create a flexible daily routine

Strangely enough, your day time routine is itself a powerful sleep association. Research shows that if your baby is part of your daily routine, he or she will develop mature circadian rhythms more quickly, and thus sleep better at night. In other words, take your baby with you on your daily activities so you are active and quiet at the same times. Studies on infants have shown that regular exposure to daylight will help your baby adapt to the cycle of day and night. It's also been shown that babies exposed to light in the afternoon will sleep better.

A daily routine may look something like this:

- Wake up. Give your baby a feed, then get dressed and head outside, weather permitting, to the playground or shops so you have some daylight and fresh air. Some 'play' in the form of eye contact, singing and chatting to your baby will also stimulate them and ready them for a good sleep later on. Activities such as baby swimming lessons or a children's session at a local library are other ways to fill your morning.

Tummy time is great for giving your baby some exercise and strengthening his neck and shoulders, and can be done on a soft rug from birth. Some babies love it, others hate it, but if you build up gradually to around 15 minutes a day it's a great first workout for your baby and will help to tire him out. Tummy time should always be done under supervision – hold a toy in front of your baby's face to keep them happy as they work out.

- Home for a morning nap
  With a very young baby, this will be only an hour or two after waking. For older babies and toddlers, it might be after lunch. You will know your baby is tired as they will start to complain and perhaps cry, avoid eye contact, and start to rub their eyes or clench their fists. Each baby has their own 'tired' signs, and you will soon start to recognise yours.

- Wake up
  Now it's time for lunch, play time, and try to get outside for a walk and some more daylight. Board books, singing, movement and chatter are other good ways to give your baby the stimulation she needs to learn and grow.

- Afternoon nap
  With very young babies, there is not much point trying to predict nap times as they aren't established straight away, and will change from day to day at first. But older babies will start to fall asleep reliably in the afternoon for a longer nap. Ideally,

Baby Sleep

they should be awake again by three, or four at the latest, if you want them to be in bed again for 7.30pm, but this is up to the individual baby.

Some babies can be up at five and asleep again by six; others will be up until 10pm if they are asleep past four pm. You will need to track your own babies sleep to work out when and how much sleep they need – we will cover sleep logs in a later chapter.

- Evening routine and bedtime
  Creating a predictable bedtime routine is key to establishing good sleep habits and making sleep training run more smoothly later on. Start with dinner, or a feed, followed by a warm bath, perhaps a massage, and then quiet time before bed with lots of cuddles, singing, a top-up feed and maybe a board book or two, then lights out at the same time each evening. Busy days with lots of attention, chatter and cuddles for your baby will "fill their cup" so they are more ready for sleep at night, too.

Please note that you don't have to live by this routine – depending on your own nature, you might prefer more flexibility. But with babies, a flexible, yet predictable routine can provide structure and security for your little one, and help you feel more in control, too.

Create a strong sense of night time being sleep time

Helping your baby understand that night time is for sleeping is crucial for establishing a good sleep routine. At night, after dinner, a warm bath can help to make your baby ready for sleep. Doing the same things before bed each night – a story, some quiet time in their sleeping room – will also ready them for sleep.

Throughout the night, too, make sure that wake times are as quiet and boring as possible to convey to you baby that *there's nothing happening here, it's time to sleep*. Minimise eye contact, and don't have any play or bright lights or screens on during night feeds or wakings (this another reason a night light can be useful).

Try not to move your baby too much if you are feeding them, as this will help them to stay drowsy. An open-sided cot bed next to yours will help you deal with night wakings with as little disruption as possible. If you need a light to see what you're doing, choose a very low wattage so the room remains as dark as possible. Black-out blinds on the windows can also help to keep your baby from waking too much during the night.

Introduce wind-down time at night, and try to stick to it

Even if you aren't following a strict routine, it's a good idea to give your baby plenty of time to wind down at night. Think of your own night time routine and how it's easier to get to sleep if you've carried out familiar rituals beforehand, such as putting on your night clothes, and brushing your teeth and maybe reading a book. Your baby will respond to sleep cues, too – it's just a matter of finding ones that work for you. These could include the following:

- A warm bath, perhaps with some lavender oil added.
- A massage in a warm, dimly lit room, with soothing oils. A bedtime massage has been shown to improve baby sleep.
- A bedtime story or two – simple board books will do. It's not so much the 'reading' but the cuddling in bed, the calming reading voice, and the familiarity of the ritual that will settle your baby.
- Skin to skin contact for very small babies, who may like to be tucked up against you in bed to fall asleep.
- A bedtime song such as Twinkle Twinkle Little Star.

- A soft, soothing stroke of the back or hand, although not all babies will like this and it may actually wake some up – you'll need to test it yourself!
- Feeding your baby right before sleep, then putting them down and waiting until they drop off, is also a way to help them fall easily into sleep.
- Feeding your baby to sleep is also an option chosen by many mothers, including me. Eventually you need to break the association with feeding and sleep, but when the time is right, it will happen. We will get to that later!
- If you don't want to get into the habit of feeding your baby to sleep, you can feed her until she is drowsy, perhaps already dressed in her sleeping bag, then settle her in her cot so that she drops off on her own, knowing you are close by but not 'needing' you to fall asleep. This will teach her that she can put herself to sleep, and may make things easier in the long run. As with everything, though, you will need to work out what your particular baby prefers and go along with that, to some extent. More highly strung or clingy babies may resist being put down in their cot to sleep and will only fall asleep in your arms – there's nothing wrong with this, particularly in the early days, so don't let anyone tell you you're "creating a rod for your own back" – everything can be changed when the time is right.

Ensure the temperature is right

An overheated room isn't great for sleep quality or for safety. Body temperature changes throughout the day, and once we fall asleep it naturally drops. Ensuring your baby's body temperature drops off at bedtime will encourage a deeper sleep, and can also help them fall asleep faster. If the temperature is too hot or cold, the baby's body will try to regulate it, and it will take longer for sleep to descend.

Baby Sleep

The ideal temperature is between 68 and 72 degrees Fahrenheit (or 19 to 21 degrees Celsius.) If it's hard for you to achieve this in your house, dressing the baby suitably is the next best option. As I have already mentioned, sleeping bags that your baby wears are the safest and most reliable option for good sleep – you can buy them in varying tog thicknesses to suit your particular climate and time of year. Generally, go for a thick tog in winter, a thin one in summer, and dress your baby in a sleepsuit underneath that covers his or her feet. You will soon work out what's best for your baby, and if they are overdressed they will look red and fretful, and feel hot to the touch. If your baby's chest or belly feel sweaty, remove a layer of clothing or dial down the heating.

The right temperature is also essential for safety. The risk of Sudden Infant Death Syndrome, or SIDS, increases in winter when babies might be bundled up under too many blankets and overheat.

Create darkness

As with all people, babies cycle between periods of wakefulness and rest, but unlike adults, they have no way of controlling this for themselves. When they get overstimulated and tired, they need to transition into an environment of low stimulation so they can fall asleep. One of the best ways of doing this is to create a room that is very dark. This is easy at night, and in the daytime you can achieve it with a blackout blind that can be placed over your window with plastic suction cups. As soon as your baby sees the dark room they will begin to anticipate sleep, their muscles will relax, and they will begin to feel drowsy. And indeed at any time of day when your baby gets upset or overstimulated, taking them to a quiet, dim room will help to calm them down.

Minimise noise and use white noise, if necessary

As with bright light, too much noise can be overwhelming for babies, who will become overstimulated and find it even harder to drop off.

Baby Sleep

Obviously you can't create a perfectly soundless environment, but you can use white noise within your baby's sleeping area to block out other sounds.

White noise can reduce stress, encourage deeper sleep, and reduce any overstimulation. You can buy white noise generating machines, or use an app on your smartphone. It's important, though, that the white noise isn't too loud (no more than 50 to 60 decibels), or too close to the crib. And while it can be helpful for some babies, it may not work for all of them. But it's worth a try! If you want to phase it out eventually, you can just dial it down a little each day until it's off.

A table or ceiling fan is another sleep aid that can be helpful, both for the monotonous sound and for the air movement, which can promote a restful sleep.

What is a Sleep Log?

Some parents like to track their baby's sleep on a sleep log. This can be as simple as a notebook, or you can use an Excel spreadsheet or even an app to record your baby's sleep. Logging the length and timing of your baby's night sleeps and naps may help you identify a pattern to their sleep, and keep track of just how many hours of rest they are getting. This may be useful to show your child health nurse, or to simply get a better understanding of your child's need for sleep.

You will also be able to note changes over a longer period of time, and perhaps get some comfort from the fact that your baby's sleep is gradually improving. And a sleep log may also help you work out just how much sleep your baby needs to be happy and alert during the daytime, if you look back a day or two and note just how much sleep they have (or haven't) had, and compare it with their behaviour.

Sometimes, paying attention to their sleep can solve certain problems. For example, my son would go to bed at night easily as long as he was awake from his afternoon nap by no later than 3pm. Any later than

Baby Sleep

that, and he would be up until 10pm. So I would always aim to have him down for his nap by 1.30pm, and around 3pm I would start gently making a little noise and allowing him to wake up. Once you work out how your child's sleep works best, you can plan around your 'best practice' findings accordingly.

While a sleep log won't work for everyone, it's useful to keep track of your baby's sleeping patterns, and will help you feel more in control, too. There are even shareable online apps that you can use to log naps and other information, which you can share with other caregivers looking after your child.

Chapter 3 - Baby Sleep Problems

8 Common Baby Sleep Problems by Age & How to Manage Them

Newborns and small babies

At this age, you have to accept a degree of disrupted sleep. It will pass, but my best advice is to give yourself a break. As I've said earlier, take all the help you are offered, don't give yourself a hard time about a messy house or a takeaway dinner, and know that it will soon be over and everyone will be sleeping better. Just rest, enjoy your newborn and recover from the birth and pregnancy. It's honestly not for long. Having said that, there are a few sleep issues you may come up against that you may want to address for safety reasons or just because they will make your life easier and aren't difficult to fix.

- Not being able to sleep on their back

At this age, it's recommended that babies are always put to bed on their backs, as any other position increases the risk of SIDS. One solution is to swaddle babies firmly in a blanket to help them feel more secure and stop them flailing around. Another is to rock them gently to sleep, then move them into their bassinet or cot once they are deeply asleep. If you are consistent, she will eventually get used to sleeping on her back.

- Not knowing the difference between night and day

As we have discussed, babies have no sense of night or day, and wake frequently throughout the night to feed. We've looked at ways you can start to give them a sense of night and day, which will help over time. These include going outside and getting some natural light in the daytime, and keeping nighttime wakings as dark and quiet as you can, so she gets the message that darkness is for sleeping.

- Hunger

If you are breastfeeding, be sure to keep in touch with a lactation consultant to ensure that your baby is getting a good feed, as a hungry baby will find it hard to sleep. Breastfeeding can take a while to establish, so in those early days you may need to hold your baby or feed for a long time to get them off to sleep. Always get as much help as you need and you can look forward to better sleep once the feeding routine is established.

With bottle-fed babies, again, ensure that the baby is getting enough food, checking the instructions for mixing the formula up carefully. A warm bath, followed by a feed, should ensure a good sleep.

Two to three month old babies

- Sleep regression

Around this age your baby should be sleeping better, however you may also notice a sleep regression. This often accompanies a growth spurt or development leap, and is characterised by an alert, active baby who shows no signs of wanting to sleep. There's not much you can do apart from work on solidifying your night time routine – bath, story, bed – so that your baby gets the message that nights are for sleeping, not playing. It will soon pass, but if it's exhausting you, see if you can get some extra rest or naps in the meantime. We will look more at sleep regressions later on.

Feeding through the night is another habit you can fall in to, especially with breastfed babies. Your baby feeds little and often, leaving you exhausted. If you keep your baby in your room with you, you may be able to manage night feeds without fully waking up. But if you would like to stretch out the time between feeds so you get more sleep, try and give your baby a really good feed last thing at night, and perhaps express a bottle of milk so your partner can take over one feed (although this may be more hassle than it's worth, and some breastfed babies will simply refuse a bottle and hold out for the breast. Creating set times for bottles or breastfeeds in the daytime and trying to stick to them may also guide your baby towards a more regular sleeping and feeding pattern through the might.

- Teething pain

Some babies may seem unsettled when they have a tooth coming through, with red cheeks and drooling. Extra cuddles, a teething ring and a warm bath will all help to settle him. Teething will generally pass quickly, but if your baby seems to be particularly unhappy, a visit to your family doctor is worth a try, as they may recommend some baby painkillers which will help with sleep, too. Having said that, teething can also be used as a catch-all term for any unsettled behaviour – sometimes, it's worth looking a little deeper to find out if there's any other solutions to usettled behaviour.

Four to five month old babies

- Overstimulation

Around this age your baby may drop a nap, and start sleeping less in the daytime. This may lead to her being overtired at night and harder to settle. It's important to realise that an overtired baby may 'fire up' and become much more active, loud and energetic, rather than sleepy. This can be a sign of overstimulation, so if your baby seems overtired, try starting the bedtime routine a little earlier with all its associated sleep cues so they can catch up on sleep.

My second son used to "flap" himself to sleep, discharging extra energy by pumping his arms up and down. Even now, at six, he will do a bit of gymnastics before bed. It doesn't mean he isn't ready for bed, though, so I will firmly guide him to his bed at the right time and he will fall asleep within minutes. Babies and children often fight sleep – but don't let them win!

Baby Sleep

Sometimes, with an overtired baby, it takes longer for them to wind down, which can create a vicious circle of another late night followed by another unsettled day. It may help to 'break the cycle' with a busy afternoon that includes some play and outside time, followed by a good feed, a long bath and an early bedtime. No matter how alert your baby seems, keep in mind ideal sleep quantities for each age bracket and aim to get them – very tired children won't learn and thrive as well as well-rested ones.

Six months

- Still waking up wanting a feed

Although we don't remember it in the morning, we all wake up during the night a couple of times, and fall back to sleep again almost immediately with no memory of the event. Babies need to learn to fall back to sleep as well, preferably on their own and without requiring too much help from their caregivers, past the age of about six months.

If you've been feeding your baby to sleep, you might now consider moving this feed to thirty minutes before bedtime, and following it with a board book story and some lullabies in bed. You can expect some fussing at this change of routine, but if you are consistent, she will drift off without the bottle or breast if she is tired. This will hopefully also make night wakings easier – if she learns that she can get back to sleep without a feed, just your voice and perhaps a gentle stroke should be enough to settle her again.

Of course, if you don't mind feeding through the night, don't feel you have to do this. But if you are exhausted during the day, it might be a good idea to introduce some gentle sleep training around six months to make day-to-day life easier. There will be much more on this later!

- Early waking

Some babies wake early, raring to go. You can try adjusting naps and bedtimes, or put a black-out blind over the window to try and push her wake up time back a little. Another option is to bring her into your bed and hope that she drifts back to sleep.

Ultimately, though, early mornings are part and parcel of having a young baby, so getting to bed earlier yourself so you can handle the early start may be the best solution.

Fixing Less Common Reasons for Poor Sleep

Sickness

Unfortunately sickness – an upset tummy, an earache, a cold – can all result in terrible sleep. Keep on hand a baby painkiller recommended by your doctor or child health nurse so you can administer it when pain strikes in the middle of the night. Hopefully, the illness will pass quickly and sleep will return. But when this happens, you may have to simply accept a disrupted night and hope for some respite the following day. We will cover more on handling sleep problems caused by sickness later on.

Travel or a change of routine

Even now that my kids are older, I accept that the first night in a new place is going to be difficult. A change of routine, the excitement of a new environment and possibly a long nap on the journey will all result in a bad night's sleep, or a late, drawn-out bedtime. However, by the second night, everyone should be exhausted and sleep well.

Travel with babies can be difficult for this and many other reasons, so my suggestion is to manage your expectations and take things easy. Travelling with children does get easier as they get older, and more fun, particularly once everyone can read and swim. But in the early days, it's not always relaxing or even worth the hassle, a lot of the time.

At these times, if you have some kind of a routine or structure that is familiar to your baby – such as a warm bath, followed by stories in bed – you can always return to this to give your child the signal that it's time to sleep. Extra cuddles and lots of reassurance will also help.

At times of disruption – travel, growth spurts, developmental leaps – a familiar routine is a great way to keep things on track until everyone adjusts to the new reality.

A new caregiver or starting daycare are other things that can cause your baby to be unsettled and fussy, often just when you need them to be 'good.' Remember, your baby isn't trying to make your life harder, they are just unsettled and need you to show them that everything is fine.

Personally, I have always been a huge fan of stories in bed with my babies and young children. It is a nice way to unwind together at the end of the day, and as your child grows it will help them with talking and learning about the world and using their imagination. Plus, reading to your children will set them up very well for school later on – any time you give it now will pay off later.

Only sleeping while being held

This is a tricky one, and some trial-and-error is required if you want to break this habit. Often, introducing a white noise CD while rocking or holding your baby will give her another sleep cue. After a few days, you can try putting her down while playing the white noise, gently patting, rocking or shushing until she is asleep.

Sometimes babies need to know you are there to fall asleep. So if you are trying this, stay with your baby until he is deeply asleep. Shush, pat, rock – do anything apart from lie down with your baby or pick him up. He may object, but will soon learn that he can fall asleep without being held, as long as he knows you are there. Once he has

Baby Sleep

taught himself to drift off, you will be able to leave the room earlier without too much trouble.

An overtired baby that finds it hard to get to sleep

If you get to know your baby's signs of tiredness – rubbing eyes, grizzling, sometimes clenched fists – you will know to put them down at the first sign, if you can, before they get really exhausted and overtired. Sometimes, though, you miss that magic moment and it becomes harder to get your baby to sleep as they are so worked up. Sometimes, a pram or a car drive can help as the movement lulls them to sleep. Or staying with them in a dark room until they drop off is another way to break through the overtiredness and allow sleep to arrive.

Only catnapping for short periods of time

Some babies will only sleep for twenty minutes then wake up again, still seeming tired. In this case, go back to basics and look at your whole sleep routine and environment. Is the room dark, quiet and the right temperature? Are you putting her down soon enough? Putting a baby down to sleep when they are already overtired can make it harder for them to reach a deep sleep. Also, look at your nighttime routine – are you following a set pattern each night, with afternoon play and daylight, a good feed, long bath and set bedtime? Putting in place a firmer structure can help some babies adjust and sleep better. Sometimes, though, it's just a matter of getting through until they learn to sleep better, and if this is the case, you may need to look at ways to cope with less sleep, which we looked at earlier one.

Falling asleep in the car or the pram

With some babies, they may fall asleep while you are out, and you'll find that when you get home and attempt to put them into bed, they wake up again, missing their nap. If this happens to you, it may be easier to not disturb them once they are asleep. If they are in a pram, simply wheel it somewhere quiet and keep an eye on it until they wake up. If you are in a car, park somewhere shady and pull out a book or your smartphone, keeping the air-conditioning or heating on depending on the weather. If you take snacks and drinks with you when you are out, you can simply enjoy nap time in your car. But never, ever leave a sleeping baby in a car unattended.

What Your Baby's Sleep Habits Mean

If your baby finds it hard to fall asleep

They may be overtired or unsettled for some reason. In this case, it's often good to start bedtime earlier, and see if that helps. An overtired baby will find it much harder to get to sleep.

They may be hungry. Around six months, when your baby starts eating solids, they may suddenly start to sleep much more deeply. You can also try introducing high-fat, dense foods to satisfy their hunger. Toast with lots of avocado and butter, for example, is a dense, high-fat food that will fill your baby up. Another good food is pureed chicken soup – the protein is very filling.

They may be having a growth spurt or developmental leap, or unsettled for some other reason. More on this later.

Unexplained unsettled behaviour

Unfortunately, there is never a 'one size fits all' solution when it comes to baby behaviour. Nor is there a set of guidelines that will solve all of your sleep problems. What you can do is understand what is normal behaviour and also keep in mind that the tricky phases will pass with time. Sometimes, just ensuring you get enough downtime by cutting back on other activities if you are feeling worn out is the best solution. Whatever your baby is struggling with usually won't last for long, and as time goes by your sleep will return.

Other strange sleep habits

Snorting and snoring

Babies make all sorts of funny noises, and snorting or snoring during sleep is nothing to be concerned about. Babies may also snore gently when they have a blocked nose. A vaporiser or humidifier in the room, or sitting with your baby in a steamy bathroom, may help to clear their nasal passages and make them more comfortable before sleep. Having said that, a baby who snores all the time, not just when under-the-weather, is worth seeing your doctor about, as it may be a sign of a health problem. Your doctor may refer you to a paediatric ear, nose and throat specialist for further tests.

Heavy sweating during sleep

Some babies tend to 'run hot', and you will notice that they sweat a lot while sleeping, particularly during their deep sleep and sometimes soaking their sheets. Because babies spend 50 per cent of their sleep time in deep sleep, if they sweat during this time, it will tend to be more noticeable. Always check the temperature of the room and ensure your baby is not overdressed, as overheating can be a risk factor for SIDS.

You should also mention excessive sweating to your doctor, as it can be a sign of an underlying health issue. Don't feel you have to pile your baby with blankets – they will let you know if they are cold, and you can also check how warm they are by feeling their hands or chest.

Of course, babies can also simply get very hot in summer. If you're hot, your baby probably is too. A warm, but not hot, bath and perhaps a clean wet flannel to suck on in the bath can ensure your baby stays cool and hydrated enough to drift off to sleep. But if the house feels cool and your baby is not overdressed yet still feels very hot, talk to your doctor.

Rocking and headbanging

Babies may sometimes get on all fours and rock in bed. It looks strange, but it's totally normal, particularly when they are drifting off to sleep. Babies also sometimes practise new physical movements while half asleep, again and again, until they finally lie down and sleep. Keep an eye on your baby if they are doing this in bed – it's quite fascinating! – but don't worry too much. It may be accompanied by head banging or rolling – again, weird, but totally normal. This often happens around six to nine months, when babies start to master new skills around movement and crawling.

Head banging may also be a distraction from the pain of a tooth coming in, and can continue for some time. It's rarely a sign of anything serious, but it's worth mentioning it to your doctor, especially if your child is showing any other signs of developmental delay.

Teeth grinding

Many babies grind their teeth, especially during sleep. It's also common when the first tooth comes through. It sounds awful, but isn't anything to worry about. You can, however, mention it when you take your baby to her first dental appointment, at around one year of age.

Chapter 4 - Preparing for Sleep Training

Sleep training is something that you might want to consider when you and your baby are both ready, if you feel desperate for sleep and want your baby to learn to drift off to sleep on her own. While it doesn't work for all babies (or parents), I believe that it's a reasonable approach that can have a positive impact on family life. Yes, there might be a few days of crying and broken sleep, but an exhausted parent who is waking every few hours to pat, rock and feed a baby is not ideal in the long-term, either, particularly if it's affecting your mental health, happiness levels, work and relationships.

Bear in mind, though, that you don't have to sleep train if you don't want to. If you can live with broken sleep, and find ways to manage, such as co-sleeping or napping when your baby naps, you don't need to do anything. It's up to you, and you should always do what feels right.

If you don't want to sleep train, simply continue with your bedtime routine and other strategies for night waking we have already outlined, and work around it until your baby is sleeping better, or you decide that the time is right for sleep training. You might choose to keep the baby's cot next to your bed, or place a mattress in the baby's room, or alternate 'on duty' nights with your partner until your baby is better at getting through the night without waking.

Ultimately, as with everything to do with looking after a baby, you can look at the research and current information, take what you can and decide what will work for you and your family. Before we dive into the nitty-gritty of sleep training, though, we need to look at what it is.

We'll also cover how to work out if your baby is ready for sleep training, and how to choose the right sleep training method for your baby.

Hard Truths about Sleep Training that All Parents Must Know

Sleep training, sometimes (wrongly) referred to as 'crying it out', is essentially teaching your baby how to fall asleep on their own, or with limited help.

You can go in to the room periodically to provide reassurance – patting, stroking and soothing – but you don't pick the baby up or take him into your bed. The aim is to 'train' your baby to fall asleep independently, without all the rocking, cuddling, bottles, breastfeeding and other sleep aids you have been using.

It can be a divisive issue. Some people believe that you should never leave a baby to cry, that you will do untold psychological damage, and that you should simply go along with what the baby wants. Child development experts don't always agree on whether it's an appropriate solution to poor sleep. But what we do know is that it's possible to introduce some sleep training in a gentle way, without simply closing the door on your baby and leaving them alone until morning. In the old days that was known as the 'crying it out' method, and we have definitely moved on from that! Here are some things you need to consider when deciding to sleep train.

Sleep training doesn't always work

Whether you follow the old-fashioned (and no longer recommended) path of leaving your baby alone until morning, or try a more gentle approach, be aware that success is not guaranteed. Both methods work with some babies, but not all of them. Some will put up more of a fight, and you may have to accept this and remind yourself that in a few years they will be in their own beds and sleeping well. And that when they are teenagers you will struggle to stop them from sleeping at all, and you will perhaps long for their baby days!

Bear in mind, too, that for around 20 per cent of babies, sleep training simply doesn't work – they may be too young, or not able to cope with separation from their parents. Like so many parenting scenarios, it comes down to your child's unique temperament. And yours, too – you may find that you can't cope with the sound of your baby screaming for you in distress, and abandon the idea on the very first night.

It's not something you need to beat yourself up about

Some parents find it incredibly hard to make the decision to sleep train, worrying that they are being cruel or causing their baby long-lasting emotional damage. What you need to keep in mind, though, is that in the setting of a loving, safe family environment, sleep training is unlikely to do any lasting damage. And in fact, if you are returning to work, looking after other children or driving regularly, it's essential for you to get a good nights' sleep too, for safety reasons and for your own mental health and wellbeing. So please don't beat yourself up about wanting to change your baby's sleep habits. Sometimes, for the good of the wider family, it's worth at least trying.

Bear in mind, too, that once upon a time, parents had much more family support to draw on, with grandparents and other family members stepping up to help with childcare and quietly appear in the small hours to give exhausted parents a break. Plus, these days, many women combine work with childcare, so need to be alert and busy during the day.

Today's families also tend to be much smaller and more contained, and nearby family help or help from older siblings is not always available. What this means is that problems with sleep fall squarely on the parents' shoulders (often the mother's). It's not unreasonable, in today's pressured parenting environment, to work towards a good night's sleep!

It's a good idea to address sleeping problems sooner rather than later

With babies and children, the longer you leave a particular behaviour unaddressed – whether that be thumb sucking or falling asleep in front of the TV – the harder it is to eventually change it. So if you lie down with your baby every night, or feed them to sleep, they will get used to it and not want to change. If you don't mind, it's fine – you don't need to change anything. But if you want to spend less time at night on bedtimes, for example, you're better off addressing it head on rather than waiting and hoping that things will change by themselves. Chances are, if the baby likes it (and if it means being close to you, they will) they won't change without a bit of a struggle. There will be some pain and crying while you put in place the new habits, but if you are firm, consistent and determined, the pain will be short lived and you can look forward to everyone having better sleep and your evenings back. As a parent, you are in charge, and if you are consistent, your child will come to the party eventually. They want to please you, after all.

There is no set formula that is guaranteed to work

Some sleep training books will offer a very structured approach to sleep training, but what you need to remember is that the authors don't know your or your baby. So what works for some babies won't work for others – and it doesn't mean you're doing anything wrong. What you need to look for is what some researchers call the 'magic moment' when your baby will stop crying and gradually drift off to sleep. This may be due to lots of reassurance and visits from parents, or your baby may do better if you remove yourself from the room for a little longer between visits.

Baby Sleep

You will work this out yourself, and you may be surprised to discover that your baby needs a bit of time to do some 'unwinding' crying on their own, knowing you are nearby, in order to get to sleep.

Even now, my pre-schooler son will often fall asleep faster if I leave him alone, even though he may call for me. If I go in, he wants to chat and engage with me, and the whole process takes longer. Eventually, you will work out what helps your particular baby. You'll also be able to tell the difference between a falling-asleep, not particularly distressed cry that is simply the baby unwinding and releasing pent-up stress before sleep, and a seriously distressed, anxious cry that is not going to result in sleep any time soon.

It's important to remember, too, that some crying in babies, toddlers, children and even adults is healthy. A good cry relaxes us and discharges emotions and tensions, so don't feel that you are doing your child any harm if they are left to cry a little. Sometimes, it's simply part of their falling-asleep process, and helps them to relax and wind down. It's only a problem if you leave them to cry alone for hours, or ignore any serious distress. A calm, relaxed approach, with some gentle words of support, is the best way to handle sleep training.

What you definitely don't want to do is to try sleep training, abandon it, then try again, on and off for an indefinite period of time. This is unfair on your baby, as they don't know what you want from them and they won't know what to expect from bedtimes.

Your baby may sleep better after training, but there will still be bad nights

Sleep training isn't a miracle solution, and it's not about solving all of your baby's sleep problems for ever. It's more about improving matters so that ideally your baby can drift off to sleep independently, and you feel more rested in general.

You will still have nights when your baby needs you – perhaps they had a bad day, feel unwell, or they are going through a growth spurt or developmental leap and need some extra reassurance. There's no harm in going to your baby in the night when they cry out for you – that is simply part of being a parent. It doesn't mean you need to pick her up or bring her into your bed, though, unless you want to. Once you've done some basic sleep training, your baby should generally be able to get back to sleep with a few gentle words and a reassuring stroke from you. And if you have an unsettled night due to sickness or some other reason, return to your routine as soon as possible so you don't undo all the progress you've made.

In summary, it's up to you – and in the context of a loving home, many child health experts believe that some gentle sleep training is worth a try if you are feeling exhausted and irritable.

Is Your Baby Ready for Sleep Training?

Around six months is a good time to think about whether your baby is ready for sleep training. Before this time, it's developmentally appropriate for your baby to be waking in the night for a feed, and they can't really be 'trained' to sleep for longer. But if you decide you want to try and change things, don't wait for too long after this point, and sleep habits will be more established and harder to break.

By six months of age, a baby will be used to you picking them up and rocking them back to sleep, and perhaps feeding them, too. But if you feel you would like more sleep, then there is nothing wrong with trying to change things a little. So if at this point you decide you would like to try sleep training, it may be that over a period of three or four nights of some crying, you will find that your baby is settling and sleeping much better.

Baby Sleep

So when is sleep training recommended? Read on for some common reasons to try sleep training.

If your baby is waking through the night to be fed.

Here, you may not mind feeding your baby through the night. There's nothing wrong with doing so, particularly if you are breastfeeding and your baby is close by, and you can feed without either of you waking up too much. But if you are still waking through the night to heat bottles and your baby requires soothing and rocking to get back to sleep, it's not unreasonable to at least try to change things at this point.

Around six months is a good time to try this – your baby is likely to be much more settled and relaxed, and you have gotten past the initial shock of a new baby. If you feel you'd like to push for a bit more routine around sleep, give it a go.

If your baby is unable to drift off to sleep alone

Again, this may not be a problem for you. But if you have other children to look after, or you simply want your evenings back and would like your baby to be able to fall asleep independently, trying some gentle sleep training may be a good idea. Single parents and parents of twins may also need to try sleep training sooner for practical reasons.

As your baby gets bigger, rocking to sleep can become harder, so you may find that your aching arms make the decision for you! The end result will ideally be that you carry out your usual bedtime routine, as we discussed in earlier chapters, settle your baby in bed, and he or she falls asleep independently, perhaps with a little 'wind-down' crying. And you get your evenings back!

If your baby is sleeping longer at night already

Once your baby is bigger, and eating three meals a day, and sleeping well at night, you may consider sleep training to move your baby into better long-term sleep habits. If waking up to breastfeed or have a bottle in the middle of the night is no longer necessary from a nutritional point of view, but seems more like a habit, you may choose to train now.

If your baby shows some ability to self soothe

If your baby seems relaxed in general, and falls asleep easily without seeming fretful or distressed, you may want to try sleep training now. Some babies are temperamentally more highly strung than others, but if you feel like your baby will respond well to sleep training, and you are generally happy with her development, there's no harm in giving it a go at six months of age. You can always try again at nine or twelve months if it doesn't work. If you're really lucky, you might end up with a baby who prefers to drift off to sleep without any extra attention. Though if that's the case, you probably won't be reading this book!

The timing is right for your family

Addressing disrupted nights and trying to get your whole family sleeping better is going to take a few nights of disruption, effort and willpower on your behalf. Factor this in, read up on sleep training, and plan your approach and time so that you have the best chance of success. Don't sleep train when you are busy at work or with other activities and need your rest. Make sure you don't have other things on, such as visitors coming to stay or a holiday away from your home and routine. Nor should you attempt to sleep train when your baby is sick or otherwise unsettled with some new change in his routine, such as starting at a new daycare.

Choose a time when everyone is well and happy, and you can give it your full focus for a few nights. If it doesn't work, so be it. You can always try again in a few months time.

Baby Sleep

How to Choose the Right Sleep Training Method for Your Baby

There is no one sleep training method that is guaranteed to work. Research shows that they all achieve around the same degree of success, but it will depend on what works best for your child and his particular temperament. The most important thing is to be consistent. The four main methods are "Cry it Out", "Fade Out", "Pick up Put Down" and "Camping Out."

And there's the final method, that you may find, eventually, is that the best thing for you and your family is to co-sleep with your baby, because he or she demands to be close – up to you. You can always try sleep training again later.

As I've mentioned, by the time your baby is around six months old, you'll have some idea of his temperament. In fact, you'll get a sense of his personality as soon as you meet him, but by six months you should know whether he's a fretful, clingy baby or a more relaxed one. Does he need to be close at all times or is he happy for periods alone? Is he determined to always have his own way, or does he show some flexibility? All of these factors will help you decide what kind of sleep training to use.

The first thing to work out is if you need to sleep train at all. If you are lucky, you may have a baby that can naturally self-soothe. Try this test: put your tired, well-fed baby to sleep and let him cry for a little while. He may drop off to sleep quickly all by himself, in which case you don't need to sleep train at all – lucky you!

But it's not always so easy. Generally speaking, a very sensitive, highly strung child will need a slower approach, or may not cope with sleep training at all.

A more strong-willed child may need a firmer approach, and be left to fall asleep largely on his own with a few nights of crying, because a parent coming into the room will strengthen his resolve to fight back against the new system!

Other, relatively easy-going babies often respond well to more gentle "No Cry", "Fading Out", or modified cry-it-out methods.

You also need to think about your own temperament: do you have the resolve for a fast, cry it out sleep training programme over a short period of time, or do you feel more comfortable taking longer to sleep train, but doing it more gently? Sleep training can be particularly hard when you are already sleep deprived, and for any parent, the sound of a crying baby is quite unbearable.

Plus, you need to think about other people in the family. Will children be woken by late-night screaming? Do you have a partner who can help share the burden of sleep training? You are looking at a minimum of three nights of disruption, with many babies taking seven to 10 nights before they are fully on board. So plan your strategy accordingly.

Ready to dive in?

In the next chapter, we'll give you a range of sleep training methods to try, from gentle training to faster methods that you carry out over several nights. We'll also look at what you need to do to succeed, and what happens if it doesn't work.

Chapter 5 - Sleep Training Success

4 Transformative Sleep Training Methods

Before we dive into the various sleep training methods, it's important to understand that there are no guarantees. And, as with everything to do with babies, there is no one answer. What you may end up using is a combination of the methods described below. You may find, once you start, that even two minutes of crying is unbearable for you, and choose to opt for a more gentle method. Always follow your own instincts here, and never do anything that makes you feel bad. But also try not to feel guilty about a bit of crying. It honestly won't do your baby any permanent damage. Permanent harm to children comes from things like abuse, war, food shortages and homelessness. So remember to keep the issue of sleep training in perspective!

It's developmentally normal for babies to cry before sleep – it helps them to discharge stress and tire themselves out, and you are not a 'bad parent' if you decide to try and get more sleep or help them fall asleep on their own. Remind yourself of the overall benefits of everyone getting more sleep, and also that famous parenting manta, "This too shall pass." An exhausted parent is not good for her baby either, and if you are returning to work or have other commitments, such as other children, it's perfectly reasonable to try and get your baby into better sleep habits.

Before you start, remember to implement a semi-regular day routine, with enough interesting and varied activity that your baby is left tired but not completely exhausted. Try and incorporate a walk or outing, some daylight, some 'play', a visit to a new house or relative, and lots of chatter and singing, etc, as well as three healthy and filling meals. Naps should be regular and ideally not too late, as if your baby is overtired he will find it harder to settle.

This busy day can be followed by a set sequence of pre-bed rituals, as mentioned earier – a warm bath, perhaps a massage with some lavender-infused baby oil, a board-book story or two, a lullaby, lots of cuddles, and zipping your baby into his sleepsuit. Keep the lights low, turn the TV off, and make sure there is nothing interesting happening in another room that your baby will pick up on and want to investigate!

All of these rituals will send the message to your baby that it's time to relax and sleep, and make sleep training run more smoothly. If you have been feeding your baby to sleep, you can try breaking this association by feeding before stories and sleepsuit, rather than at the end. Keep calm yourself throughout the bedtime ritual, even if you are desperate to get the baby to sleep so you can have some time to yourself. Your baby will always pick up on your mood, so if you seem agitated or impatient, it may take longer to get him drowsy and drifting off.

Essentially, get your daytime house in order, including daytime naps and a bedtime ritual, before you try and tackle nights. We will cover naps more in an upcoming chapter.

OK – let's now move on to the four most common sleep training methods, and the benefits of each.

Fading out method

This has a number of names, but I'm calling it the Fading Method here. Essentially, with this method, you put your baby down to sleep after his normal bedtime ritual, and leave the room. At this point your baby will usually cry for you, but rather than go in immediately, you wait for a minute or so, before going back in to soothe, reassure and say a few gentle words. But you do not pick up your baby.

Gradually, you increase the amount of time you are out of the room, stretching it by a minute or two, until you are out of the room for 10-15 minute at a time. Ideally, your baby tires himself out and drifts off

Baby Sleep

to sleep. If this method is going to work, it should do so within a week. Some people find that this method distresses the baby more, as every time you reappear in the room you upset the baby once again. Others find that it works well and after a few days to a week their baby is falling asleep with minimal crying and distress.

This is the standard method that works best for most parents, so it's the one that I cover in detail later on. Other methods are simply variations of this one – some more gentle, one more dramatic. But this is the one I strongly recommend you start off with, and then adapt depending on your baby's response.

Cry it out method

Also ominously knowns as the Extinction Method, this is the classic method that most people think of when they hear the words 'sleep training.' It may also be called 'controlled crying.' This is essentially putting your baby to bed and not returning for a long period of time, sometimes even until morning. It's hard on the baby, who may become very distressed, and it can be hard on parents too. Generally, I think it's better to accept that you are going to have a few nights of disrupted sleep attending to your baby and hopefully they will sleep better at the end of it. Most parents would find it very difficult to fall asleep to a screaming baby, anyway.

Pick up Put Down Method

This method is similar to the Fading Out method, in that you go in and out of the room for gradually lengthening periods of time. It differs, though, in that instead of reassuring your baby with words and strokes, you pick him up to soothe him, before placing him back in his cot. For some babies, this extra holding makes them feel secure and they will eventually drift off to sleep. For others, though, being picked up and put down will over time make them overstimulated and distressed, and they will fight sleep harder.

It can also depend on how you are feeling – if you find yourself getting agitated and upset by your baby's crying, he may pick up on that and become more distressed himself.

This method is, however, quite gentle, so you can start it with babies who are just a couple of months old. It may work from a very early age, and if it doesn't, you can simply try again a little later.

Camping out method

This involves being in the room, sitting on a chair, to offer reassurance, but not picking up your baby, rocking them, or feeding them. Gradually you move the chair further and further away until you are out of the room. The baby knows you are there, but gradually learns to fall asleep on her own.

This method can be used when others have failed, but can be distressing for parents if your child becomes very upset and you feel that you 'shouldn't' pick him up. However, it does mean you don't have to leave your baby alone to cry, which some parents find unbearable.

Another option here is to set up a pull out mattress next to your baby's cot, so they know you are there but can't really see you or engage with you. You can take the time to have a rest while they drift off to sleep (or bring in your smartphone, as long as your baby isn't distracted by it) and then simply tiptoe out once they are asleep. However, you may question how successful this is as your baby is still using your presence as a 'sleep aid'. It's not easy!

Sleep Training in More Detail: Here's How

I will now cover the Fade Out sleep training method, which you can adapt based on how your baby responds. This gives you a basic method to follow, but is in no way prescriptive – you'll have to adapt it to suit your temperament as well as your baby's. This is the one that trains

Baby Sleep

your baby, but more gently than the traditional Cry It Out method, and seems to me the easiest on both the parents and the baby.

Here's how to do it:

1. Get your baby into his own room

If you are starting sleep training at around six months, it's fine to allow your baby to fall asleep in his own room while the training is taking place. If your baby has been in your room up until this point, leave him there, but relocate temporarily to another part of the house or apartment yourself, even on a mattress in your living room, if you have nowhere else. Once your baby is sleeping better, you can move back into your bedroom.

If your baby has been sharing a room with an older child, move the older child into your room or another room for five nights or so (let them know that it won't be forever, just until the baby is sleeping better). Once the training is over, the child can move back in with the baby – and in fact, this often works very well for young children, who like having a sibling in the same room as them.

2. Remove all sleep aids

If you want your baby to learn to sleep, you will need to remove everything that they currently use to get back to sleep. This includes pacifiers, bottles of milk, rocking and patting and breastfeeding. Babies who have learned to sleep will still wake in the night from time to time, but won't require a bottle, breastfeed, pacifier or anything else to get back to sleep. If you want a good night's sleep, all of these aids have to go, or you'll continue being woken in the night for 'room service'.

3. Plan your approach

Sleep training should ideally take place once you have worked out a plan and talked it over with your partner, so you are both on the same page. Also, if you have close neighbours, let them know what's going on so they don't assume the baby is being left to cry. Pick a time that suits you, when the baby is well and you don't have other things going on.

4. Ensure you are well and happy, too

Don't try sleep training if you are under lots of pressure at work, or don't feel happy about it for some reason. Sleep training requires calm, confident parents, so get some extra rest in preparation, and make sure you are feeling calm and positive before you start. Think Calm, Confident, Consistent and you are on your way to better nights! If you are going to be falling apart, crying and feeling guilty, it's best not to even try sleep training, as it does take determination!

The First Night

Carry out your bedtime ritual as normal around 7.30pm, ensuring your baby has been up since at least 4pm, preferably earlier.

Put her to bed without any sleep aids. She will cry, but stay out of the room for a few minutes, then go back in and provide some brief reassurance, such as a stroke of the cheek or some gentle words, then leave again.

Remember, she now needs to get herself to sleep.

Go back in to your baby as often as you need to, but gradually lengthen the intervals until she falls asleep. Be prepared for some resistance – this may take an hour, or perhaps two, and there will be a lot of crying and yelling. Remind yourself of the benefits of everyone getting more unbroken sleep at night, if you feel yourself wavering.

She will also wake up during the night, particularly if she is used to having a breastfeed, bottle or pacifier. Rather than getting up and down all night, get out of bed when she wakes again, maybe have a cup of tea or watch some TV, and wait until she goes back to sleep again.

There may be quite a lot of crying on the first night. But by the third night of sleep training there will be less, and your baby should be sleeping well within five nights, after a small amount of 'wind-down' crying at bedtime.

How to Make Sure Your Baby Sleeps Through the Night

Once you have been through sleep training with your baby, you will naturally want to make sure it continues to work. The best way to ensure your baby does a lot of sleeping and very little waking at night (allowing for the odd disruption due to sickness or a developmental leap, for example), is to stay consistent. Here are some ways to make sure your baby sleeps through the night.

Don't reintroduce sleep aids

As part of your sleep training, you removed all external sleep aids, such as pacifiers, bottles of milk, and breastfeeding. Now that you have done that, don't reintroduce the pacifier or other aids, as it will only confuse your baby and set you back.

Babies who have learned to sleep on their own, without any external help, will continue to do so, and should make it through to morning without disturbing their parents at all. This may make daytime sleeps harder for a week or so, but they will soon improve too.

Don't change their nappy during the night

Once your baby is asleep, leave them be. There is no need to change nappies during the night.

Don't panic if they vomit

Sometimes, a baby may vomit during sleep training. This is no reason to give up, as babies do vomit very easily at times. If it happens, stay calm, clean your baby without too much fuss, and continue as you started. As long as you remain calm and consistent, your baby will quickly calm down.

Why Sleep Training Fails & What to Do

Sometimes sleep training simply doesn't work. This can be due to the baby's temperament or the fact that you simply can't bear to leave your baby to cry. Here are some common reasons for failure, and what you can do about them.

- Your living arrangements aren't suitable

If you have a very small apartment and share a room with your baby, it may be difficult to leave your baby to cry. Neighbours and other people living in your house who disagree with what you're doing can also make it hard. There are no easy answers here - you may need to wait a little longer, or work on sleep training your baby a little more slowly, with less crying. Options here include rocking, patting, a dummy and breastfeeding through the night, for example.

- Your baby puts up a strong fight

Some babies will react very strongly to sleep training and giving up their sleep aids. In some cases, this may mean that it takes longer. In others, you may feel that the crying and protests aren't worth it. It may take as long as seven days to see results, but as long as you are following the guidelines I have outlined above, and your baby doesn't seem to be getting more distressed, you can continue.

Baby Sleep

It may also be that your baby isn't ready. In this case, wait until he is a little older, perhaps nine or 10 months, and then try again.

- Lack of support from those around you

Sometimes sleep training fails because one parent isn't on board with the idea, or perhaps because other people, such as well-meaning friends and family, try and tell you it's a bad idea. If you can't come to a suitable compromise, or feel yourself wavering, again, it may be better to leave it for a few months and try again later. As always, listen to your own instincts here, as they will serve you better than well-meaning outsiders who don't understand your baby or your situation as well as you do. And have a chat to your health care provider if that helps.

- Lack of planning or it's just not the right time

As you can see from reading through the programme, you need to factor in a certain amount of broken sleep and disruption when sleep training. If you try and do it at a time when you have a lot of other things happening, or you haven't factored in how much energy it will take, it may not succeed. Again (are you seeing a theme here?), let it go if it's not working or you can't handle it right now, and try again later.

Personally, I don't think it's worth doing too much sleep training before six months of age. In my experience, you will get better results if you wait until your baby is eating well during the day, and more settled generally. Before then, managing on less sleep and adapting your lifestyle accordingly is a better option.

- Lack of consistency

If you let your baby into your bed one night, then the following night refuse to pick them up, and then give up after two hours, then it's fair to say that you aren't going to successfully sleep train your baby.

Remember that babies don't find it easy to understand what you are trying to do, so being consistent is essential if you want a new habit to stick. They will go along with what you want eventually, but they need to know what that is.

- You haven't got the day sleeps under control

If you don't have consistent day sleeps, you will struggle to implement any kind of routine at night. As I have stated earlier, always work on your daytime routine and your bedtime ritual before you try and tackle nights. If this is fairly consistent, sleep training should be much easier.

- Your check ups are too stimulating

When you go into to check on your baby, take care not to be too over-the-top in your attention. Remain calm and reassuring, but keep your visit as brief and simple as possible so that you don't overstimulate or further distress your baby. You want him to feel safe and reassured by your presence, but also able to put himself to sleep – a tricky balance, and one that may be easier with your second baby, if you have one.

Chapter 6 - It's Naptime!

Good day sleeps are another important need for babies through their first year. The patterns of napping will change and eventually your baby will have their own established routine. Getting this right, and prioritising naps so that they don't miss this important rest time, is key to good sleeping at night.

One question new parents often ask is if naptime can interfere with bedtime. Generally, no. While a very late nap – for example, waking up after 4pm, can lead to a later bedtime – for most babies, good naps during the day mean they aren't overtired at night and will find it easier to drift off to sleep.

If you get your baby down for his afternoon nap at time that allows for two 45-minute sleep cycles and a wake-up time of around 3pm, you should be fine for bedtime. And, of course, some lucky parents have a baby who can sleep until 5pm and still be back in bed by 7pm.

Babies change so quickly throughout their first year, and that 'good sleeper' you bring home from the hospital will soon be awake much more, and need more help to get back to sleep for daytime naps. Read on for a guide to how many naps your baby should be having throughout their first year and beyond.

Newborns (up to six weeks of age) should be having three to five naps a day, with 30 to 90 minutes awake time between each nap. There will be one nap in the morning and one or two in the afternoon, with perhaps a couple of short 'catnaps' thrown in, too.

Babies from six to 15 weeks of age should be having three to four naps a day, with one or two hours of awake time between each nap.

Babies aged four to six months need three naps a day, with lengthening awake times of 1.5 to 2.5 hours between each nap.

Babies aged six to eight months need two to three naps a day, with two to three hours of awake time between each nap.

Babies aged eight to ten months need one to two naps a day, with two to three hours between each nap. Generally, babies who wake very early (between five am and six am) will keep having two sleeps for longer. If they sleep a little later in the morning, they will transition to one sleep a day more quickly.

Babies aged 10-12 months plus need one to two naps a day, with 2.5 to 3.5 hours of awake time between each nap.

After the first birthday, your baby may continue to have two sleeps, but many will have a single, longer nap after lunch, and this can continue until they are aged three or even four. But some toddlers will drop their day sleeps quite early, which can be disappointing for parents who rely on that time to get a few things done and enjoy some peace and quiet. Read on for a few strategies to deal with babies and toddlers who refuse to nap.

Strategies for a Successful Naptime

When your baby is very small, naps will happen without you needing to do much more beyond feeding, cuddling and soothing them to sleep, perhaps in your arms or close by in bed.

You may wish to try and get them into a routine, but many parents find that their naps and awake times change so quickly that by the time they are used to one routine, their baby no longer plays along – such as when the morning nap is dropped.

Once they are around six months though, when they are settled, eating three meals and day and moving more, it can be a good idea to time daytime naps more precisely so that your baby is up and busy again well before bedtime. And, as I've mentioned earlier, sorting out your day time routine is essential for successful sleep training at night at this age.

Here are some key ways to ensure that naps are successful:

Pay attention to your baby's natural sleep cycle, and time naps accordingly.

Look for signs of tiredness – rubbing eyes, signs of unhappiness, clenched fists, avoiding eye contact – and move your baby towards their sleeping area before they get really upset, feeding first to fill them up before sleep.

Have a designated sleeping area and take them there once they are ready to nap. We have covered this already, but it should be warm but not overheated, dark, quiet and peaceful. Putting your baby to sleep in the same place for every nap may work well for babies who 'fight sleep' as it sets up strong sleep associations and signals to them that it's time for bed.

For daytime naps, a blackout blind may be helpful in encouraging your baby to drop off, and some parents swear by a strict nap schedule (for example, at 12 noon every day for exactly) to ensure that the day nap happens and bedtime isn't disrupted. As with many things, only you will be able to work out what will suit you lifestyle and your baby's temperament and sleep patterns.

Others may fall asleep in the car and readily transfer to a pram or their own bed. With my first son I used to let him fall asleep in the car, then move him gently to his pram and let him have his sleep there, so I could go to the library or a cafe and have some time to myself. This worked for me, but it won't work for all babies and toddlers, who may struggle to 'transfer' to a pram or their own bed during a nap.

Choose what works for you and your baby – the time when they are asleep is a well-deserved break for you, too, so ideally you want them to get a good, long sleep at this time so you get a break, too.

Leave them alone to fall asleep - as with sleep training at night, you sometimes need to leave your baby alone for a few minutes to actually drop off to sleep. Some babies need time to unwind and fuss a little before dropping off, so leave your baby to it and see what happens. If your baby becomes distressed, you can try picking him up, soothing etc, and then try again to put him down, drowsy and relaxed, but still awake, to see if he will fall asleep on his own.

Be consistent. Working your day around your baby's naps takes some planning, but can make life much easier. Get out and about when they are awake and happy, then be home for naptime so that they get a good long sleep and you get some time to yourself. Knowing when they need to be down for their nap so that they get a good sleep but are still up in time for their evening routine and set bedtime means that night sleeping will fall into place more easily, too.

Don't let them nap for too long, or too late. Some babies are still confused about night and day, and will sleep for too long during the day, then be alert at night. Try to limit late afternoon naps from around six months of age, getting them down for sleep earlier so you know they will have time to get through the early evening and bedtime routine without dropping off again.

While I don't believe in waking a sleeping baby (why would you?) I think it's worth timing naps so that you have some consistency when your baby will be ready for bed at night. This also ensures that your baby is getting enough sleep, which is so critical for development.

What if Your Baby Won't Nap?

Some babies and toddlers will go through tricky phases when they won't nap during the day, no matter how exhausted and grumpy they

Baby Sleep

may seem. Sometimes, this can mean you need to look at bedtime and move it a little earlier or a little later and see if this helps. And some days are just more challenging than others.

If your baby hasn't had enough stimulation or exercise they may resist naptime. Here, some activity can help, such as going for a swim in a heated pool, or to a playground or playgroup. Lots of chatter, singing and engagement with them will also ready them for a good sleep. Being consistent, remaining calm and keeping an eye out for sleep cues may also help. As soon as your baby seems relaxed and drowsy, take him in to his sleeping area and see if he will drop off.

Also, some babies and toddlers will stop napping at around one year to 15 months, apart from perhaps the odd catnap. This does make the day long for parents, but if it's what your baby chooses, there's not much you can do about it. Encouraging 'quiet time' after lunch can mean you still get a break – leaving them in their room with an audio book playing, or with a few books and toys, for example. And ideally bed time will be earlier if your baby or toddler has been awake all day.

Signs that your baby or toddler is ready to drop their daytime nap are generally that the child simply refuses to sleep, even if you put him in his cot. He may play, scream or cry out. And after a week or so the parent realises the nap is not going to happen. There may be a week or two of unsettled, overtired behaviour, but eventually you and your child will both adjust to the new routine.

You may also decide to stop the daytime sleep yourself if your baby is up until 9pm at night and you are no longer getting any time to yourself in the evenings. You may choose to live with this, or you may decide to drop the daytime nap in exchange for an early bedtime – it's up to you.

If you do have a baby who doesn't sleep during the day, I recommend pursuing a sleep training programme at night. You may not be able to force your baby to sleep during the day, but that is all the more reason to assume that they can and will sleep well at night. Often, sorting out night time sleeping can help with day sleeps, too. And even if they don't, and your baby or toddler has definitely given up their day nap, or only has brief catnaps, at least everyone is getting a good sleep at night.

Remember also that so many of these problems will vanish in a few years' time and you won't even remember them. Your children will be at school, come home exhausted, and fall into bed without too much drama. So don't despair too much if you have a 'bad sleeper' – it's not your fault, and it will pass!

Chapter 7 - No Problem Too Big

In this chapter we'll cover the dreaded sleep regressions that occur as your baby moves through babyhood and toddler months. They aren't as scary as they sound, they, and will pass quickly. But until they do, there are a few things you can try that will make life easier in the meantime.

We'll also look at how to work on establishing good sleep habits when you are parenting alone. And finally, we'll cover sleep when you have twins. In both of these scenarios, parents need extra support, and there are ways of making it easier for yourself.

Understanding Sleep Regressions by Age

Sleep regression is something you will come up against a few times as your baby moves towards toddlerhood. It's totally normal, and is characterised by your baby waking up frequently when previously she had been sleeping well. Daytime naps might be difficult; you might feel like you've barely had any sleep because she was up and down all night, fretting and crying. Your baby might also seem grumpy, fretful and more clingy than usual.

Sleep regressions tend to last from about two weeks to six weeks if you're unlucky. Although sleep regression can be difficult, especially if everything has been going well up until that point, they are part of your baby's rapid development at this time, and means that they are healthy, thriving and growing as they should be.

Sleep regressions mostly occur at four, nine, 18 and 36 months of age – which are also times when your baby is changing rapidly and going through a lot of physical and cognitive development. One thing you will notice is that babies and toddlers don't change gradually – they seem the same for a while, and then all of a sudden they may be eating more, seem unsettled, or sleeping deeply, and then you'll find they have changed quite rapidly, thanks to a big growth spurt. One of the biggest transformations is around the age of three, when your toddler transforms into a very small child – and this stage is also characterised by a final sleep regression.

While not all babies and toddlers experience dramatic sleep regressions, most parents do notice a change in sleeping patterns around these ages, and it helps to be prepared for it. Read on for more information about sleep regressions by age.

The Four Month Sleep Regression

This sleep regression is when babies change from their newborn pattern of active sleep followed by deep sleep, into a new pattern of cycling through REM, light and active sleep. You may notice some unsettled behaviour and clinginess, some poor sleep at night, and also greater focus from your baby – he or she suddenly seems more alert, and more like a person. This is a lovely age and a small sleep regression won't matter so much when you noticed so much more joy and engagement from your baby!

The Nine Month Sleep Regression

The regression at nine months occurs at around the same time your baby develops "object permanence," which is the understanding that someone or something still exists even if your baby can't see them. This can also cause some separation anxiety, which is why your previously happy baby will now weep when you go to the shower, for example. Even if you have successfully sleep trained your baby at around six months, she will now wake up and realise that you're not there and start to cry, wanting you to be near her.

Let her know that you are leaving the room and will come back, rather than suddenly disappearing. This will make it easier for her and help her understand that when you go, you always come back. This may make nighttime separation anxiety less troubling, too.

Around this time babies also have a significant growth spurt as they move towards toddlerhood. They will start standing, crawling and moving around. You may notice your baby practising these skills in a half-sleep state, which obviously interferes with bedtime. Be assured, it will pass! And once they are on the move, they will sleep better at night, too.

The 18 Month Sleep Regression

This is another period of rapid change for your toddler – he or she is becoming more independent and starting to think about how he relates to others more. With a new social and emotional awareness comes increased anxiety and perhaps some disrupted sleep.

The 36 Month Sleep Regression

Much like the regression at 18 months, this period in your toddler's life is characterised by a huge leap in development and growth, both emotional and physical. Your little one may be starting pre-school, and is also likely to be talking lots, moving lots and spending time with other children more. New emotions, such as jealousy, can also take time to work through, particularly as this is often a time when a new sibling appears on the scene.

Toddlers are also learning a huge amount right now – which can make it hard for them to settle down to sleep. The world around them becomes fascinating – everything from leaves to worms to water is a source of constant information, and you'll be hearing the word 'why?' a lot, too. Dreams and imagination are taking off, along with fears both rational and irrational.

All of these factors can increase anxiety and lead to some unsettled nights until your child settles into his new 'self.'

How to Deal With Sleep Regressions

If your baby is very young, you will need to provide extra reassurance and cuddles until the sleep regression passes. Look after your own needs, too, until your baby is more settled, and get more sleep and rest as needed, much as you did when your baby was a newborn.

If you have already sleep trained at around six months, try not to abandon everything your baby has learned. Ideally, you will provide extra care and soothing as necessary, without moving them into your bed, or giving up on letting your baby drift off to sleep alone permanently. While it may not feel like it at the time, sleep regressions do pass. Staying in the room a little longer may be all you need to do to help your baby through this stage.

If you do end up co-sleeping or cuddling your baby to sleep for a while, you may need to do some sleep training again once the regression is over – see how you go. Some tummy or head stroking, with some soothing sounds and your presence, may be all that's required, keeping to your routine of putting your baby down drowsy, but awake.

As always, keep the sleeping area dark and quiet, to give your baby the clear message that it's time to sleep. Now is a good time to demonstrate, again, that nights are a little boring, too – turn off all screens, and ensure that there's nothing too interesting happening in your house at bedtime.

Sometimes, checking in on your baby during the night and offering a stroke and a kiss may reassure them that you are there, preventing more upset later.

For sleep regressions in older babies and toddlers, also ensure that they are getting plenty of time during the day to practise new skills, such as gross motor skills. Set up an "obstacle course" in your home for them to crawl and climb over, or take them to a baby-friendly play centre and let them do some exploring. Giving them lots of opportunity to work on new skills and wear themselves out in the day time can make a big difference to your nights.

You'll also need to offer more emotional support during the day. She's feeling more adventurous and independent, but this can lead to some anxiety too. Extra attention, lots of cuddles and cosy time with books and a blanket will all make a big difference. Give her opportunities to discharge all that emotion with laughter, play and even some tears while you hold and soothe her – she'll be much happier after a good cry.

The main thing to remember is that your baby will need some extra support at this time, and the more you are able to offer, the easier and more smoothly the sleep regression will go.

If In Doubt, Seek Help

As always, if your instincts are troubling you, see your paediatrician if you feel like the sleep regression is going on for too long, or your child seems really distressed. Talking to your doctor will rule out any larger problems, and help to set your mind at ease.

Look After Yourself

If you are feeling exhausted by your child's sleep regression, be sure to cancel any unnecessary commitments and get some extra sleep yourself. As always, you need to fill your own cup up as a parent before you can take care of your child's needs properly. So eat well, have some early nights and soon it will pass.

6 Must-Know Sleep Strategies for Single Parents

If you are parenting a baby alone, first of all know that my heart goes out to you! Read on for some sleep strategies to help single parents get through those early weeks with a newborn, and through the times that follow.

Call On Help

If you can, call on family or friends to help you get through the early months with your baby. Just having someone take the baby from you for a few hours so you can get some extra sleep in the mornings will make a huge difference to your energy levels. If you can afford it, a night nurse will also be invaluable in helping you through the newborn stage. Or even someone who can come in during the day and hold the baby for a few hours, or walk it around the block, while you have a rest or just stare into space.

Gather a Support Network

If you're a single parent, you'll have times when you are managing fine, and times when you need a bit of extra help, for example when you get sick. Work on building up a reliable local support network within your community so that you can call on someone when you are having a bad week, and return the favour when they need help from you. Join online community groups, go to mother's groups, and ask your local child health centre about what kind of support is available to single parents in your area. If you have space, an au pair or student who can help out a little in exchange for accommodation is another option that may work for you.

Sleep When Your Baby Sleeps

Baby Sleep

Easier said than done, I know, particularly when you have lots of other things to do in your spare time. But worth doing for your health and your energy levels. If you don't want to sleep through every nap time, just do it when you can. Or once or twice a week, go to bed at night when your baby does, so you can catch up on sleep that way.

If you find it hard to sleep during the day, at least try and enjoy your free time when you can. Rather than doing housework, call a friend, or have a relaxing bath, or read a book with a cup of tea – whatever you need to unwind.

Consider Whether Co-sleeping Might Work For You

As we have discussed in earlier chapters, co-sleeping can often work with clingy babies who don't like to be separated from their parents. If you think this is a good idea, try setting up a cot next to your bed with an open side so your baby has a safe place to sleep, yet is still close to you. This will make nighttime feeds and wakings much easier when you don't get a respite or have someone else to share the night feeds.

Get To Know Other Single Parents

You'll soon find other people in the same position as you, who can sympathise with the challenges of lone parenting. Find groups online or in real life where you can have a laugh and talk and share tips without judgement. You're not alone – you just need to find your community! The great thing about online communities for parents is that they are global, so there's always someone to talk to, even in the middle of the night.

Be Aware of Your Mental Health

Single parenting is a tough gig at times, so it's important to be vigilant about your own health and wellbeing. Know the signs of postpartum depression, and keep in regular contact with your family doctor. Always seek help if you find yourself struggling. Keep a list of phone numbers for parenting helplines and health services close to and so you can always get support, should you need it.

Working On Your Baby's Sleep as a Single Parent

Much of what we have already covered remains the same when you are parenting alone. But here are some tips to help you with your baby's sleep that are both realistic and will make life much easier for you.

- A simple, manageable bedtime routine will help you feel in control. While this is helpful for all parents, I think it's particularly important for single parents who will find the routine stops them from being overwhelmed – and of course it's great for lone parents to get some time to themselves in the evenings, so don't feel bad about putting your baby to be early and sleep training at six months, should you need to!

- Have a sleepover with a relative or friend who can give you a break from early morning wake-ups. Ideally, it should be someone who will help out with some light housework, get up early or in the night, and provide some emotional support. One day, you will return the favour, so take all help that's offered! It's important to ask, as sometimes people don't really know what you need. And again, seek out any support services on offer within your community, too.

Baby Sleep

Two Babies, Many Solutions

If you have twins, you may be wondering if you can try sleep training at all. After all, if it's difficult to get one baby to sleep, how on earth will you manage with two? As with lone parenting, you may find that establishing and following a set routine makes it easier for you to manage this added responsibility. And again, don't be afraid to ask for help, including from local services set up to support families with twins and more. Also, take heart. While teaching two babies to sleep might seem much harder, you can and will get there. Here are some tips, often sourced from parents who have raised twins themselves.

Set the Same Bedtime for Both

What you want to do here is synchronise your babies' sleep cycles so that they are awake and asleep at around the same times. Otherwise, one or the other will always be awake, and you will soon be exhausted. Fortunately, twins are naturally in tune with one another, so here you can work with their natural inclination to be close. The principles here are much the same as sleep training single babies.

Always Settle The Calmer Baby First

You probably know this already, but if not, always work on your calmer baby first, to allow you uninterrupted time with the fussy one a little later. This will mean your calm baby gets your attention and hopefully drifts off to sleep, and therefore doesn't miss out on the attention her or she needs.

If one starts fussing, check on the quiet one first to make sure she's happy, then deal with the fussy one. This will help both babies to feel loved and happy. And don't panic if one starts screaming – often, twins aren't bothered by the other one's cry, even if they are in the same room.

Put your twins to be when they are awake, but drowsy

Here again, you can start some simple sleep training even when your twins are quite small by putting them into their safe sleeping space when they are still awake. They will hopefully drift off to sleep, leaving you with some much-needed alone time. You won't be able to rock two babies to sleep for long, so putting your babies down to sleep is going to be a decision that is made for you, to a certain degree. You can still give them cuddles while they are awake, perhaps a couple of board books and a lullaby, and soon they will learn to drift off on their own, in their own bed. Ideally your partner should be around to help with bedtimes in the early months.

Try Swaddling Your Babies

Swaddling can work well for all babies, but is particularly helpful when it works for twins (I say when, because not all babies like being swaddled.) It makes babies feel safe, 'held,' and ready for sleep, and they are after all used to being very tightly packed into a small space! You will need to stop at around two months of age, but at this point you can swap to zip-up baby sleeping bags for the same sleep association and secure feeling.

Keep Nights Boring and Quiet

As with all babies, you want to discourage them from seeing night as anything other than a time to sleep. During the day, cuddle and talk to them as much as you like. But keep night-time interactions, light, cuddles and chatter to a minimum, so they are clear on the fact that nights are not play time. This is important with all babies, but particularly important with twins, when you have two babies to settle, not just one. Twins may also like a cuddly toy or some comfort object to hold onto at night from around one year of age.

Black-out blinds, lullaby CDs and white noise machines are another thing that may twin parents find very handy when getting two babies to sleep. Draw on everything you can find, and you'll find it much easier!

Accept That Your Twins May Have Different Sleep Needs

If you find that your twins sleep differently, which is common, you may need to treat them differently. Some parents put their twins in separate rooms, as one is a better sleeper than the other. As with all aspects of parenting, as long is it's safe, it's up to you. One waking up is always better than two waking up, so whatever works!

You may need to separate them into separate rooms to sleep train at around six months, and then put them back in the same room once you've managed this and they are sleeping well again. Or you might get them to sleep each night in separate rooms and then move them into one room later on in the night – up to you. The sooner you get them sleeping in a way that will work for you all long term, the better for your family as a whole. As always, go easy on yourself and ask for help when you need it.

With daytime naps, it may be that you need to soothe one to sleep first, and then the other, so one wakes around around 20 minutes earlier than the second. This is part of life with twin babies – to some extent you need to be flexible and let go of expectations. You just need to do everything one baby at a time and be patient. It will get easier!

Set Up A Sleep Schedule

More so than with one baby, with twins it's absolutely critical that parents are getting enough sleep. It shouldn't be one person getting up to do all the night wakings, it should be both. Setting up a timetable or schedule will help to ensure that no one becomes too sleep deprived. Obviously you'll need to take into account the needs of your own family, and work commitments.

Call in Help

If you can afford it, get some help, particularly in the early days. A night nurse, a cleaner, even someone to cook a few healthy meals – whatever it takes to get you through. A live-in au pair is another option that can work well.

Online parenting forums specifically for twins are another invaluable source of tips and support, as are multiple birth associations, so get on board with all of these as soon as you know you are expecting twins.

Streamline Everything

Have as much done in advance as you can – for example, bottles sterilised, nappies stocked up, sleeping bags laid out before you bring each baby out of the bath at night. Meal plan, have a weekly online shop, get regular help… whatever it takes to simplify your life! And be sure to schedule in some time for yourself, too – when you are parenting twins, this isn't a luxury, it's essential.

Chapter 8 - Completing Your No-Cry Toolkit

In our final chapter, we'll look at some common problems that come up with babies, and how you can work through them. These include how to soothe a crying baby – giving you lots of hints and strategies. We'll also look at colic – what it is, what helps, and how you can help your baby work through it. And finally, we'll look at how you can help your baby sleep better when he or she is not feeling well.

How to Soothe a Crying Baby

Learning to soothe a crying baby is something you learn on the job, and when you have a baby who cries a lot, it can be very tough on a new parent. You may wonder what's wrong with your baby, or that you are going to lose control and harm your baby or that you aren't connecting with your baby. I remember fearing, as a very new mother, that my baby was scared of me and that was why he was crying! It can feel like a rejection, but it really isn't. It's simply your baby getting used to being in the world. Once you establish some basic feeding and sleeping routines, and your baby is a little bigger, it will all get much easier.

In the meantime, learning a few techniques to soothe a crying baby will help you get through the bad days. Firstly, let's look at why babies cry so much, as this knowledge can help parents feel better able to manage it and not feel overwhelmed.

So why do babies cry so much?

All babies cry. But in truth, no one can say for sure exactly why babies. It may be to do with hunger, or bellyaches, or overtiredness. They can't talk, so they can't tell us exactly what the problem is, unfortunately. Crying is their way of gaining our attention and focus, which they need to survive when they are so small and helpless. But over time, you will learn to recognise some of your baby's unique crying patterns and what they mean – and then you will be able to meet their needs so the crying soon stops.

And in fact, it's important to remember that a healthy baby should and will cry regularly. If your baby never cries, you should seek advice from your family doctor.

Some common reasons for crying include:

- Tiredness and overstimulation; need for sleep
- Needing a new diaper
- Feeling hungry
- Colic, reflux or food intolerances
- Pain or sickness
- Gas
- Fear or a sudden loud noise may lead to crying
- No apparent reason

As a parent, it can be hard to deal with a crying baby for hours on end, particularly when you are tired and emotional yourself. But a certain amount of crying is completely normal for all babies, and some cry a lot more than others.

What you need to bear in mind, too, is that excessive crying can be very hard on you as a parent, especially if you are someone who tends to be quite hard on yourself. You may feel that you 'should' be able to deal with your baby and you are doing something wrong if you can't stop him crying. But in fact, by simply being there, holding your baby and letting him know you are there, you are doing everything right. The early days and weeks where there may be a lot of crying will soon pass and in the meantime, you just need to go easy on yourself and get as much rest as you can. Unexplained crying builds from birth, tends to peak at about six weeks of age, and tapers off by three months. Mark your calendar and look forward to that magic date when the crying stops – it will come.

Having said that, if your baby seems like they are in pain, or you sense that something is wrong, always seek medical help. Trust your instincts.

Baby Crying Patterns by Age

Birth to three weeks: At this age, many babies sleep a lot and cry for only short periods of time, usually due to hunger or tiredness.

Three weeks to 12 weeks: At this point, babies tend to cry more and sleep less. There may be some periods of crying due to hunger or overtiredness, which are easily solved with sleep, a feed or some gentle soothing. And there may be some periods of unexplained crying where nothing seems to help. For some babies, there is a lot of crying, for no apparent reason, that goes on for a few months, often until three or six months of age. This occurs with around 20 per cent of babies, unfortunately. By six months, most babies are much happier and more settled in the world.

Often the diagnosis is 'colic', which is a kind of catch-all term for the unsettled crying and apparent stomach pain that many babies seem to show when they crying a lot, writhe and howl after feeding. Often, there may be more crying in the evening, that can go on for a couple of hours before sleep descends. And sometimes there may be a bad day when it feels like your baby does nothing but cry.

Here are some effective remedies for colic that you may find useful. There are no proven treatments for colic, because the causes can be so hard to pinpoint in individual babies, mostly because they are so young and change so quickly. But you can try and lesson their discomfort and distress so that the episode passes more quickly, and in trying different things you may be able to pinpoint what is causing them it to some extent.

5 Effective Remedies for Colic

Lay your baby on his tummy

You can do this across your lap, on the floor on a rug, or more upright along your chest. You can also gently rub his back, which might help with any digestive discomfort. Tummy time will also help to strengthen neck and shoulder muscles, but you should only do this when your baby is awake and you are there to keep an eye on him or he

Work on good sleep

Of course I would say this! But it's true – sorting out good sleep is the key to sorting out a lot of your baby's unsettled behaviour. And very small babies have an added difficulty in that they find it hard to 'hold still' enough to go to sleep, often jerking themselves awake as they drop off. Swaddling, rocking and even "wearing" your baby in a sling are all ways to hold them still enough to soothe their distress and let them fall asleep. Another trick is to walk the floor with your baby – wrap them up or put them in a sling, and the pace up and down until they drop off. If you know they are well fed and there aren't any underlying health issues, it's fine to wear headphones may block out the crying until they fall asleep.

Another problem is of course that babies can only stay away for a short period of time before they get grumpy and restless, and they then need to calm down enough to fall asleep – but are crying too much to manage this! This is something that they will learn to do over time, and meanwhile they need your patience and support.

Introduce a pacifier

Baby Sleep

You may find that your baby is much happier and able to calm themselves down with a pacifier. Yes, you will need to get rid of it at some point, but many parents find it gives them some much needed relief from crying.

Give a warm bath before bed

A long, warm bath will often calm a crying baby – the water, the sounds and the soothing hands holding them will all help to settle colic and fretful behaviour. A massage in dark, warm room with a scented oil, some cuddling, and gentle white noise may also help to soothe a colicky baby.

Gentle handling

When your baby is very unhappy and colicky, be sure to handle them with firm, steady movements, without any jerking or hard back-patting. Sharp movements will alarm your baby and cause more screaming and upset. Another reason small babies become upset is if they are handed between lots of different people. Sometimes, if your baby becomes overstimulated retreating to a dark, quiet room can help. What they need more than anything is a calm, safe environment with you. They have just arrived in the world, after all, and it can be frightening.

Oddly enough, some parents report that holding their baby a lot during the day gives rise to easier evenings. Babies love being held, rocked, and close to you, so if you leave them in their pram all day they may "hand you a bill" later and demand a few hours of your undivided attention in the evening. If you find you have a very clingy, colicky baby, a sling can help you get a few things done without having to put your baby down.

An important point: This need for attention never really goes away – your children will always want your attention, and pre-empting this need with lots of loving attention will prevent them trying to gain it with acting out, or giving up and "looking for love in all the wrong places" later on.

Manage your own wellbeing with a colicky baby

When it comes to colicky babies, it's also helpful to manage this phase (which won't last long, but may feel like it's going to last for ever) by taking good care of yourself. Ask for support and help from those you trust, who won't make comments about your howling baby, and take any food, babysitting offers or help with cleaning that comes your way.

- Do you have someone who can come over and just hold the baby for a while so you can have a shower and some time to yourself?

- Can you get a cleaner or some other help with housework so you don't have to live in a mess, which can be very stressful?

- Can you put in some headphones and let the baby cry for a while in his bed while you take a bit of time out? A healthy baby can be left to cry for short periods of time quite safely, and may even drop off to sleep if left alone.

- Look after yourself. A crying baby can be exhausting, so as always, prioritise your own wellbeing and you will feel better able to cope with your baby. Eat well, get enough rest, and avoid alcohol and smoking and you will feel better able to cope with this stage in your life.

Is it a medical problem?

Baby Sleep

No one really knows. Some babies may suffer from reflux or other stomach upsets or be particularly sensitive to a particular formula milk, or something their mother has eaten if they are breastfed. Some mothers may try eliminating certain foods, such as chillies, spicy food, coffee, garlic or dairy – there's no harm in trying and seeing what happens.

Helping a Sick Baby Get Restful Sleep

Another aspect of living with a baby that you will have to get used to is occasional sickness, at least until their immune system has built up a little. The first year of daycare can also be rough, as your baby will bring home lots of bugs and germs he hasn't been exposed to before. Lack of hygiene and a tendency to explore and put fingers in mouths also leads to lots of not-so-lovely germs being shared around. You might noticed earaches (lots of screaming and head-banging), colds, blocked noses, feverishness and upset stomachs.

Of course, most serious illnesses can be prevented by immunisation, but colds and sniffles will still appear, and can also lead to some broken nights, sadly. Often, a sick baby will be in pain and will find it impossible to sleep. Yet sleep is exactly what they need to fight off illness and recover. What you need to do is decrease their discomfort to the point that they can sleep soundly without aches and pains keeping them (and you) up.

Here are some ways you can help your baby or toddler get a good night's sleep when they are ill:

- Use a humidifier. This will ease breathing difficulties and reduce the chance of your baby waking up due to congestion.

- Use an over-the-counter painkiller for children. Talk to your pharmacist about the best one to use and follow the instructions for correct dosages very carefully. Some babies and toddlers will happily swallow a liquid treatment, others may need a suppository. Never give more than the recommended dose – keep note of how much you have given and when.
- Allow for extra naps in the daytime to make up for broken sleep at night. Extra rocking, cuddling and attention is also going to help your baby feel better, as sickness can make them miserable and clingy. On the same note, start the bedtime routine a little earlier and make sure your baby doesn't get cold when you bathe him or her – keep a towel in the bathroom and dress him there straight away to prevent chills, and make the water nice and steamy to help clear his nose. Sometimes, sitting in a steamy bathroom can help, too.
- A vapor rub on his chest can ease breathing and feels nice, too. You can make your own by mixing up four teaspoons of grated beeswax with three tablespoons of cocoa or shea butter, seven tablespoons of coconut oil and 30 drops off essential oil – ten drops eucalyptus oil, ten drops tea tree oil, five drops lavender oil and five drops chamomile oil is a lovely blend that will clear a blocked nose and promote sleep.
- Saline nose drops, available from the pharmacist, can help to clear a blocked nose, though your baby may protest loudly.
- Propping up your baby's mattress slightly, by putting a pillow under the mattress, will also help to ease a blocked nose and the pain of an ear infection. Only do this with babies that are six months old and upwards.
- Keep your baby hydrated, either with extra breastfeeds or bottles, as needed. Older babies might prefer watered-down juice or milk – whatever keeps them drinking fluid.
- If your baby vomits in bed, clean her up as quickly and calmly as you can, keeping lights low if possible. You may also like to clean out her mouth a little to get rid of the bad taste.

- Extra skin-to-skin contact is very good for sick babies, and is proven to speed up recovery. Hold your baby against your skin and remember that she will soon feel better.

Once the sickness passed

You may need to work a little to get back into your old sleep routine, but don't let all your progress be undone by a single bout of illness. Once your baby is feeling better, go back to leaving him to fall asleep in his cot, even if you've been rocking him to sleep during his illness. Babies are fast learners and you should be able to get back on track quickly as long as you remain calm and consistent.

Preventing another illness

While illness is simply part of childhood, and something you have to accept to some degree, you also want to prevent your child catching a serious illness that will affect his development. Here are some tips to prevent illness from rearing its head too often:

- First and most importantly, immunise your child according to his schedule. This is the best, and sometimes the only way to prevent serious childhood illnesses such as measles, mumps and rubella.
- Be sure to live in a smoke-free home and avoid smoke-filled areas to keep your children's lungs clear.
- Always wash your hands when you get home from anywhere. Over time, your child will watch you and will become a good hand washer on their own. Provide a stool in the bathroom so your child can access water and soap easily.
- Wash towels, sheets and all bedding frequently.
- Avoid sharing cups, cutlery and so on.
- Breastfeeding for the first 12 months is a great way to pass on your own immunity to germs that you encounter.

- Eat lots of fresh fruit and vegetables to boost immunity. Once your baby is moving onto solids, ensure their diet is full of vitamins, too.
- If your child is sick, don't go to playdates, playgrounds or public places such as libraries. Stay at home until it passes and don't spread the germs.
- Remember that childhood illness is normal and part of your baby building up his immune system – it will pass.

A final point: Sometimes, sleep problems can feel insurmountable. Let's say you've read this entire book, tried everything I have recommended, and your baby is still not sleeping well. As I have said throughout, this will change with time. But if you find you are feeling continually worried and stressed about your baby's lack of sleep, and the impact it is having on your, don't be afraid to seek help from a child health expert, such as your family doctor.

Occasionally, sleep problems can point to wider problems within the family, or even post-natal depression, and you will need to deal with these issues before you tackle sleep. If this rings true for you, and you've found it impossible to put into place a sleep training method, then perhaps you need to seek further help. It is there if you need it.

But generally, like everything to do with babies and toddlers, as long as the basics are there – lots of love, patience, support for parents and an understanding of baby and toddler behaviour – sleep should fall into place, if not straight away, then eventually. In the meantime, look after yourself at all times, because as a parent, your little one depends on your completely, and your health and wellbeing is the foundation of stable, thriving family life.

Conclusion

I hope this book has given you a lot to work with, and you now feel ready to handle your baby's sleep problems and to attempt sleep training if you feel it's the best option for your family. As you can see, there are no perfect solutions when it comes to baby and toddler sleep, and I have tried at all times to emphasise that this is a stage that will pass, and as a parent you are well-equipped to find your own ways to manage. Some toddlers and babies are just better sleepers than others – it's often a matter of luck, but you can improve things with some work and planning.

We looked first as sleep patterns by age, and what is normal for each stage. This is great for helping you see that what may feel like problems are actually totally normal and will pass with time. We also looked at how to set up a safe sleeping space for your baby, which is more important than anything else. Here we also covered sleep aids, such as monitors, night lights, blackout blinds and white noise machines, and when these might be a good idea.

Next we covered sleep associations – what they are and how to create them. And we looked at a basic routine that you can put in place to help with good sleeping, both during the day and at night. As always, a busy day and a structured, loving and fun routine is ideal for creating the right conditions for peaceful night sleeping.

In chapter three, we looked at sleep problems by age, both common and less common, and then we moved onto sleep training in chapter four, and how to choose the right method for your baby. We also covered tips for success, and how you might decide that the time is right for sleep training, such as if you are returning to work or you are simply feeling exhausted and want to tackle sleep problems a little.

We also looked at why six months is the perfect time to first try sleep training. You now know that the longer a baby or toddler is used to behaving in a certain way, such as being rocked to sleep, the more they will struggle to give it up. By the time a toddler is two, getting him to stop falling asleep in your bed, or on the couch, is going to be a lot harder. Changing the routine later on is going to involve a lot more resistance, and a lot more pain. Having said that, if you remain calm and consistent, sleep training will usually succeed at any age. It's just that six months is the first and often the best time to try it. After that, as your baby turns into a toddler, it may not be quite so easy, and your child will also be able to climb out of their cot and use their words to make you feel like a terrible parent, so it may be better to start sooner!

Next, we dived into the main techniques for sleep training – Fading Out, Crying it Out, Pick Up Put Down and Camping Out. We looked at which babies (and parents) are best suited to each method, and why Fading Out is the one that is most likely to succeed for many families. We then looked at why, unfortunately, sleep training might fail, and what to do if that happens. Often, it's simply a case of trying again later. And, remember, as always, that if it doesn't work, or you find it too hard, then you may go back to whatever you've been doing and forget about it entirely, knowing that you tried. As the parent, it's your call.

In Chapter Six we covered nap times for different ages, and why good daytime naps are key to sound sleeping at night. We also looked at what to do if your baby won't nap. Next we moved on to sleep regression, and how to handle them at each stage, and importantly, why they happen. As with so much of parenting, knowing what is developmentally normal can make it a lot easier to deal with. Here, we also looked at how single parents, and those look after twins, can manage sleep, naps and parenting in general – the two key tips here, and for all parents, are to look after yourself and seek help if you need to.

Lastly, we looked at crying babies – what crying means, how to soothe it, how to deal with colic in the early weeks. We then covered how to manage sickness and sleep, and how to prevent childhood illness as much as possible.

I hope that you now have a lot of information and confidence to deal with your baby's sleep. While there is no magic secret to great sleep in the early months, there is a lot you can do to move things in the right direction. Try not to beat yourself up, though, if you find it difficult coping on broken sleep while also trying to get on with other elements of your life, such as work and other relationships. It's normal, in the early years, to be functioning on very little sleep and not feeling full of energy, and many other parents are in the same boat. If anything, these years will teach you to be a little bit more understanding of those around you who seem tired and out of sorts – they may well have a very small baby at home, keeping them up at night.

Good luck, and enjoy the journey!

ANGER MANAGEMENT: TAME THE LION INSIDE OF YOU FOR GOOD

Discover How To Improve Your Emotional Self Control, Make Your Relationships Thrive and Completely Take Back Your Life

Table of Contents

Introduction 103

Chapter 1: Understanding the Self 105

    Discover and Understand Your Emotions of Anger 105

    Psychology of Anger 107

    Rewind, Rethink 110

    Identify the Trigger of Your Anger 111

    Admit Your Anger 114

    Face Your Anger 116

    Explore Your Fears and Insecurities 117

Chapter 2: Manage Your Source of Anger 119

Chapter 3: Take Control of Your Anger Today 130

Chapter 4: Self-Management for Better Mental Health ... 145

    Why Is a Good Sleep Important for Anger Management? 150

    Best Routines and Tips for Better Sleep 151

    Transform Your Anger into Constructive Action 155

    Into Practicing Fitness 158

    Into a New Hobby 158

Chapter 5: Tips to Handle a Partner with Anger Issues ... 161

    Maintain Your Cool 161

    Identify the Triggers 162

    Communicate in a Productive Manner 163

    Choose Your Battles 164

    Exercise Patience 165

Empathize 165
Be Respectful and Firm 166
Seek Influence Rather Than Control 167
Do Not Put up with Insulting and Disrespectful Behavior 168
Walk Away 169

Chapter 6: Dealing with Children and Family Members with Anger Issues 170
A Child with Anger Issues 170
Family Member 181

Chapter 7: Facts About Anger 182

Chapter 8: Anger Management Goals 187
Anger Management Therapy 188
Persons Who Can Benefit 190

Conclusion 192

Introduction

Congratulations on purchasing Anger Management for Men and Women: A Practical Guide to Identify & Control Anger, and thank you for doing so!

Every effort was made to ensure it is full of as much useful information as possible.

Please enjoy!

Anger has been the revered untouchable topic that few dares to address and even fewer admit they suffer from. Downloading this book, however, is the first step towards unmasking this monster that has been gnawing on the very fabric of society. It is the first step towards ensuring that you and your loved ones are free of its hold and control.

Majority of the problems in the world today can be traced back to an angry emotion; from the plastic bottle, an angry person throws into the river that ends up in a whale's stomach at sea or the child growing up without one parent because the incarcerated parent made a bad decision in a moment of anger. Every negative thing you see has originated from anger, and it is time it to do something about it.

To that end, the following chapters will discuss anger comprehensively to help you understand and address personal anger. You will also be equipped with knowledge of how to deal with angry people around you including your child, a spouse, or a family member. You will understand the anger from a psychological stand view, identify its triggers, understand how it presents itself, and realize the need to admit it truthfully. You will also receive guidance on the process of unearthing your fears and insecurities, and from which emotions of anger do these originate in most cases.

Baby Sleep

Having had a comprehensive understanding of anger and its sources, you also learn how to take charge of your mental health to prevent the buildup of stress and anxiety by getting adequate sleep, exercising, and eating healthy foods.

There are plenty of books on this subject on the market, so thanks again for choosing this one! Every effort was made to ensure it is full of as much useful information as possible. Please enjoy!

Chapter 1: Understanding the Self

Have you found yourself regretting what you did or said in a wave of negative emotion? Did you lash out at a child, a partner or a friend? Well, you were driven by anger. Many people have broken off meaningful relationships or landed themselves in the hands of the law over irresponsible things they said or did in the heat of the moment.

No matter how docile you are, you are bound to get angry at some point. Anger is a normal feeling that only needs to be expressed in the right measure and through proper channels. Since anger is quite powerful, managing it needs a clear understanding of it and proper anger management skills. Thankfully, these can be learned.

Discover and Understand Your Emotions of Anger

Anger is one misconstrued emotion. Perhaps because it is related to pain, people feel like it is wrong to experience it. Nobody likes to feel or to be around people going through this negative emotion. People avoid anger fearing that if they lash out or express their discomfort about something, others will lash back or draw away from them. In all honesty, no one wants to be around an angry person, their negative energy drains the very life out of you. However, our discomfort with anger is because we are grossly mistaken.

The wrong ideas society has about anger have caused us to perceive anger as this alien uncontrollable force that violently takes over a person and one that calls for an equally violent method to let out. Words like 'boiling up,' 'fuming', 'bursting', 'welling up' and 'blowing off some steam are used to describe the pressure and the heat that comes with anger. It is also said that it is healthier to release this violent energy rather than keeping it bottled up. However, the idea that purging is the cure for anger is highly defective.

In truth, releasing anger as we call it only intensifies, justifies, reinforces, and amplifies it. Angry people expressing themselves violently in a bid to release the emotion are likely to say hurtful words, cause destruction of property, and embarrass themselves and others, which will also aggravate those around them. When the atmosphere is ridden with negative emotions, people are barely able to come off their high emotions without help. However, once you gain a proper understanding of what it is, why it comes up and how to deal with the emotions, anger is likely one of the best emotions in a person. You are made in such a way that all of your emotions portray passion, skills and special gifts, and it is only right if you include anger among them.

To begin with, understand anger as an inherent emotion whose function is to protect and preserve you from emotional, physical, and mental abuse. Anger is also the emotion that establishes your presence, position, and dominance to the universe. It helps to establish boundaries that set you apart as an individual, as a member of a family, and as part of different social groups.

When anger is roused, it forces you to face challenges and opposition from your personal standpoint. You are able to state your position and erect proper boundaries, thereby improving your self-image and self-esteem. It acts as a trigger that restores your sense of self and helps you define yourself outside the confines of control and influence. Beyond your own boundaries, you also become angry when other people are degraded, mistreated, insulted, or any such kind of offense. It is anger that drives you to take a stand, defend them and help them reset their personal boundaries. Consider your anger sacred as it is the reset button that proves your true identity to yourself and to others.

Subtle anger also helps to define and establish interpersonal boundaries. When you know what tips off a person, you are less likely to do it to them. This maintains mutual respect and opens up communication lines as people express to each other what they like and do not like. Unfortunately, most of us are not trained to recognize subtle emotions and will wait until the anger flares up to do something about it, which makes us associate anger with pain and negative uncontrollable behavior.

The next time that you or a person around you is angry, take a moment to understand the motivation or the factors that could be driving the anger. It could be that you are trying to define your boundaries, stamp your authority, or simply prove to the people that you exist.

Psychology of Anger

As we have established, anger is a response to the pain felt when a person goes through unpleasant experiences, which means that it does not come about in isolation. However, pain is still not enough to arouse angry emotions; thoughts that ignite anger must also be present. These could be a person's assumptions, assessments, appraisals, and reading of the situations that make them believe that their counterpart intends to cause harm to them. In that case, the negative emotions are subjected to the target believed to cause them, who can sometimes be the angry person himself.

People also use anger as a substitute to avoid feeling the pain. They do this because feeling angry often feels better than withstanding pain. They do this both consciously and subconsciously. Exchanging pain for anger is thought to be advantageous because it provides a distraction. While a person bearing pain focuses on the pain he is feeling, an angry person thinks about taking retaliatory steps against those causing the pain, sparing himself from feeling the pain.

However temporal it might be, anger also saves people from having to deal with the painful reality. It is the perfect smokescreen to mask your feelings about what is happening. A situation could be frightening and causing a person to feel defenseless but getting angry is the perfect way to get the situation resolved without having to show any vulnerability. For example, in the event of death or the diagnosis of a terminal illness, being angry and blaming yourself or the circumstances adequately masks the pain of the loss of life or of health.

Becoming angry brings a sense of moral supremacy and power. It is impossible to feel morally superior when in pain but when you get angry, you are able to justify your emotions. You become angry for a cause and take a stance against those that have done you wrong. You begin to justify punishment and other negative results believing that the perpetrators deserved it. People like to be found on the right side of reason, and will likely find a moral reason to justify their anger.

Anger can be a self-sooth strategy. When angry, the brain releases norepinephrine, an analgesic (an analgesic causes pain relief or acts as an anesthetic) triggered by psychological or physical pain. When this chemical is released expressly into the body, it numbs the pain. This makes anger both a detrimental reaction and an effective coping method for emotionally vulnerable people because it helps them survive the pain. Psychologists say that this strategy sufficiently masks even the most distressful emotions such as those that are hurt to the 'core.' They include rejection, deceit, guilt, feeling ignored, accusation, powerlessness, unfitness, and feeling unloved or devalued. However, if anger is able to fend off these agonizing feelings, a person may become dependent to the point of addiction.

Psychologists also consider anger to be the shaky rail that people use to walk towards empowerment. If a person is using anger as a self-medication to overcome psychological pain, they will undoubtedly use it to overcome feeling powerless. Besides the analgesic norepinephrine that numbs pain, the brain also excretes epinephrine, a chemical that causes an energy burst through the body causing the popular adrenaline rush. This rush is what makes sudden anger attacks cause a feel-good and all-powerful feeling. Suddenly, the defenseless and destitute feelings are replaced by an intense sense of pleasure and control. This has led psychologists to conclude that if anger is able to address some of the most deep-seated issues people have every time, many people are likely to become addicted to it and in the end, it is likely to control us all.

Unbeknownst to many, anger is also a tool used in intimate relationships as a sure way to attach. Without even knowing it, people use it to maintain some distance between them and their partners. This behavior in most cases draws back to childhood where indifferent, untrustworthy, and erratic care fostered a shy, defensive attitude for the child in his adulthood. As adults, they may still yearn for secure attachments that they missed in childhood, but they are wary of expressing this desire openly fearing dismissal and rejection. They also fear that letting down their guard will make them vulnerable to jabs and attacks from their partners based on their unstable past. This is the reason why many of them to respond with anger when a partner forces them to recount their old wounds. Therefore, anger becomes a survival technique and a protective shield that keeps others from prying or forcing them to disclose any needs or feelings.

Rewind, Rethink

We have established that anger does not work alone, it originates from previous pain, and a person's assessment of the current situation. This means that anger is driven by a precise thought process. For most people, distorted thinking is a major factor in their retaining of anger. This is what causes people to differ in opinion because if one person thinks one way, another will think differently, and one event can be interpreted differently. However, if one thought process leads to this outcome, we can comfortably assume that another thought process could lead to a different outcome. Therefore, if thinking one way triggers your anger, it is likely that thinking differently may lead you to a different reaction.

It is possible for you to change your reaction to infuriating situations by changing how you think about them. Realize that you are in charge of your emotions and that no one can make you feel any of them, not even anger. You only become angry with what you think and what you say to yourself. For example, the statements "He cannot treat me this way! I will show him who I am!" do not elicit any positive energy, you are only likely to become angrier. Therefore, you can change your reaction to stressful situations by changing how you think about them without attacking other people verbally and physically, and without releasing a string of hormones that could damage your cardiac system in the long run. With a renewed mindset, instead of getting confrontational, you will prudently find a solution to the issue.

Having the same negative reaction to unpleasant results could lead you to develop chronic anger that could harm your health. This is because anger takes up so much energy and this constant withdrawal is stressful to the body. People who get angry at minor frustrations and irritations end up altering their psychological and physical wellness. It also causes recurrent arguments and physical aggression that will undoubtedly ruin social relationships and deter improvement. It is unlikely that you will climb up your career ladder by giving your boss a tongue-lashing.

Just to emphasize, it is imperative for you to know that the things we go through in life depend on our interpretation of what bombards us. If you interpret a careless or unintentional remark as a deliberate attack on your person, you will end up using the nasty remarks as a catalyst to fuel your anger. While the person could have also truly meant to put you down, it is your thoughts that will drive you to anger. To prevent this, put up a filter that separates what comes in and what happens in your mind. Do not let the ungraciousness and crudeness of others spoil your day. Be cool, think sober thoughts, you will be fine.

Identify the Trigger of Your Anger

Rather than dealing with anger and its effects, it is easier to work towards preventing the flare-up from happening in the first place. They say prevention is better than cure. To get ahead of the anger, you must understand and correctly identify its triggers. Once you do so, you will be able to respond to them better because you will be hands on.

Each person is wired differently, which means that what tips off one person may not do the same to another. Triggers are primarily dependent on the life experiences a person has had. For example, a person who was abused physically or emotionally as a child will quickly develop anger when subjected to words or actions that threaten their physical or emotional well-being.
The general understanding, however, is that people anger more easily when they are annoyed, hungry, lonely, or tired. If these feelings are present, it does not take much to tip them off.

Below are some anger triggers.

- *Disappointment and dishonesty*: Like me, most people are tipped off by dishonesty. When a person tells a lie, you will wind up upset, annoyed, and angry when the truth comes up. Others make promises and do not live up to it. You will feel also betrayed and angry when a partner cheats, a colleague uses dishonest means to bypass you for a promotion, your child lies, a boss fails to promote you as promised or some conniving person brings a false accusation against you.

- *Discrimination and prejudice*: People are treated unfairly because of their class, nationality, sex, race or ethnic group, disability, sexual orientation, appearance, and religious beliefs, among others. Only a few people like Nelson Mandela and Gandhi have been able to channel the pain and anger from discrimination and prejudice to good and transformative causes. Prejudice and discrimination, whether blatant or subtle, brings a sense of unworthiness, defenselessness, and makes a person feel small. Most people respond to it with anger, despair, irritation, and rage. Amazingly, both the victim and the perpetrator suffer the same emotions. We have seen this in the viral videos where some people call the police on others based on biased reasons.

- *Unfair treatment*: Unfair treatment will undoubtedly cause irritation, annoyance, and anger toward anyone. Unfortunately, events like this occur quite often. For example, a teacher could give you a clearly unfair grade, a boss could assess your work inaccurately, a police officer gives an undeserving ticket or someone cuts the line at the movie theatre. While you are bound to feel bad, how you express these feelings determines whether they escalate or are brushed off as nothing.

- *Attacks*: The world is a violent place and more often than not, you or a person affiliated to you will be the subject of an attack. Attacks are in the form of intimidation, child abuse, war trauma, domestic violence, verbal attacks, sexual abuse, and accidents. While some people develop anxiety and depression, others become angry. For example, the recipients of chronic abuse end up becoming abusers too, in some events. Just like in the case of discrimination and prejudice, the perpetrators of attack often suffer anger just as their victims do.

- *Self-esteem threats*: Everyone wants to feel good about who they are. Even those who suffer chronic self-esteem issues like to feel good about themselves. However, a person will threaten your self-esteem when they insult or disrespect you, reject you, criticize you, fail to choose you or embarrass you in front of others. On receiving these threats, some people increasingly loathe themselves, become sad, and others become angry.

- *Time* pressure: Our world is presently a beehive of activities. People have the pressure to increase their output and to multitask, but inevitably, there will be things that get in the way. For example, running into traffic when hurrying to get to work, having your call put on hold for a long time, a partner or a friend constantly sending you text messages while you are busy at work or having to go through thorough security checks at the airport while getting late for your flight could make you frustrated.

Below is a summary of anger triggers discussed above and others that are not discussed. This list provides a broader view of prevalent anger triggers. (Kindly copy the list and check those that apply to you.

Managing anger will start by identifying the triggers. Add any other triggers as you recognize them).
- Lies
- Misunderstandings in relationships
- Injustice
- Offensive words
- Disappointment
- Threats
- Infringing on personal space
- Disrespect
- Insults
- Distorting information
- Inappropriate Labels

These triggers will be a starting point for you to understand the things that cause a high alert in your brain, and once you have identified and understood them, you will be prepared to handle the situation better than you did before.

Admit Your Anger

When you admit something, you declare that you have full knowledge of it and are in control. Naming and admitting, also called recognition, go hand in hand. It is impossible to recognize something without giving it a name, and you only name things that are in your knowledge. For example, when you hear a very loud deafening sound in the sky, you will be very frightened and will report that you have heard a very scary loud noise. However, once you have a name for it, you are in full control of your fears. You can differentiate between the sound an airplane makes when flying overhead and the sound of a thunderstorm. Both are loud and frightening, but you no longer fear because you understand each.

This concept applies to every other thing in life. Once you name and recognize/admit it, you will have more control over it and over how you feel about it. When you admit your anger, you realize that you are angry, understand what has triggered the anger, and are able to control it.

Knowledge and admitting anger also influences how you communicate your anger. There is a splitting difference between communicating knowledge that you are angry and communicating the feeling itself. If you want to communicate your anger, you will speak like this, "You underage pothead, pack your clothes and leave my house!"

When you speak like this, you have communicated your anger, which means that you have given in to an unknown feeling, that you do not understand, and let it control you. However, if you intend to communicate the 'knowledge of anger', you will speak like this, "I feel very angry and cannot speak to you right now. Perhaps you could leave my house and we can talk about it when I feel calmer."

The first and the second statement are very different. The first only shows that you are experiencing the feeling, but the second shows that you are in full knowledge of what is going on and can still communicate what you feel. In the first example, you would expect that a person saying these things will throw things around or is preparing himself/herself to beat the child. However, in the second example, the person is probably sitting in a chair thinking about what has happened, processing his feelings, and contemplating the action to take. The second person has control over his or her feelings than the first.

When you admit your anger, you take control of your emotions, make others see that you are firm in your decisions, and avoid making unnecessary rash judgments that could cost you in the future.

Face Your Anger

I once heard the story of a woman who forgave the man who killed her only son. She visited the man in jail, hugged him, and allowed him to rent the space next to her house after he had served time. This story sounds bizarre to many people who would beg the judge to issue the man a life sentence without parole, or better yet, a death sentence. However, this is not how facing your anger works. It is likely that the woman admitted, accepted, and faced her anger before concluding that no amount of retaliation against the killer could bring her son back. This is beyond taking the high road, but yeah, it only happens when you come face-to-face with your anger and overcome it.

Anger makes you feel like you have the right to revenge without requiring you to restore or repair what has been damaged. It introduces the concept of payback, which is an urge that people get, nudging them to restore 'cosmic balance'. It is an attempt to overcome the helplessness they feel by displaying their ability to control the situation. However, a retaliatory response only provides a temporary false sense of relief and prevents you from dealing with the pain within.

A person with an overwhelming sense of entitlement is open to anger displays. To him, expressing rage is a means to acquire control and to affirm his status as a boss, a parent, a husband, or otherwise. It is an attempt to dominate. However, the higher the expectations, the more upset the person will get when demands are not met. Nevertheless, history will tell you that those who are deeply wronged often do not carry any resentment. They have learned to rewrite those feelings to avoid being swayed away from the important task or mission at hand. Nelson Mandela, while writing in prison, said that enmity and hatred is a trap laid and that when you fall into it, it becomes difficult to differentiate you and the adversary.

In not so many words, facing your anger is simply rising above it. This does not make what has been done insignificant; it only makes you realize that there are more important things at stake. It keeps you in control of your emotions so that you do not allow a moment's fury to ruin the natural course of things. When you let go of your anger, you let go of the need to take control, which brings more peace than making sure that people shape up to meet your demands. It does not mean that people will not face the repercussions of what they have done. If people are being sloppy in their job, their performance will show soon enough. However, for your peace of mind, let go, and rise above the negative emotions. You are worth the peace that comes after.

Explore Your Fears and Insecurities

Fears and insecurities bar you from understanding yourself or the situation fully. It brings paranoia and anxieties, leading you to make harsh judgments, have lofty expectations, and avoid taking positive action. You fear criticism, judgment, rejection, unworthiness, and avoid being yourself around others. You begin to assume that everything is a direct attack. You are also likely to develop unhealthy attachments to people and use them as tools to build your self-worth and self-esteem, praying that they will only see the best in you. However, everyone is bound to make a mistake and in reality, even the people you have esteemed so much will let you down.

Most people that lack confidence naturally compensate with arrogance, cockiness, selfishness, and competition, particularly in social settings. Others become combatant, defensive, and willing to blame others for their problems. They blame others for their mistakes, are roused to jealousy, and can be very aggressive. These behaviors are not the real person; it is only an attempt to hide insecurities. This is an awful way to live because it puts you to the task of constantly hiding and masking your true self.

Baby Sleep

Unfortunately, there is not a nicer way to resolve fears and insecurities than to deal with it. People say that it is all in the mind and it is true. The problem is that you think about it too much. Have you seen someone in with a disability or a deformity that they embrace? You tend to fall in love with the person and admire their life, but guess what! Most often than not, the deformity or disability was once an insecurity that the person learned to embrace and suddenly, the world loved it too. You might also have been bullied for something, but embracing it begins to radiate beauty.

But of course, if it is something you can change, take the first step today. You will be happier with yourself, your progress and will be less prone to anger. See the peace and joy that will follow.

Chapter 2: Manage Your Source of Anger

Feelings do not just come up, they must originate from an event, a person, or an object. You could trip on your way to work and the embarrassment from that could leave you tipped off all day. A surprise gift in the morning can make you jolly all day so that you overwork, however, you still end up happy at the end of the day. Since the feelings you get do have an origin, working through anger will be more effective when you can trace it.

To determine the origin of your negative emotions, do the following:

- Discover Your Past Unmet Demands

    Anger is the iceberg that signals something bigger lies underneath. Most times, when you are feeling overwhelmed, frustrated, angry and sad, it is because a need you had was not been met. The unmet need needs voicing or acknowledging, and will constantly resurface nudging you to make peace with your past. The constant tagging slowly turns into anger that is roused at the slightest provocation. It also brings up fear and anxiety that keeps you on edge, worrying about whether or not others will find out about your insecurity.

    Some people's unmet needs date back to experiences they had in their childhood. The pain from an experience keeps gnawing at them as they regret why they did not run away, speak up or take other proactive steps to stop the abuse or unfair treatment they went through. Others remain fixated on the feeling of helplessness they had while going through the terrible situations they did. This numbing pain can prevent the person from becoming an effective guardian or parent. It can also cause them to withdraw from their family forever.

The most agonizing of these pains is the pain of disappointment when let down by people who are close and were supposed to be a source of support. Many times, people that you count on to help you at a time when you are most vulnerable do not rise up to the occasion. You may have heard of stories where children were being abused and when they reported it to their parents, the parents dismiss it or simply do nothing to stop the abuse. Others are forced to raise themselves and their siblings while their parents are out high on drugs and alcohol. Children raised by uncaring parents and in volatile environments like these do not get to experience parental care and love, and the void that forms from this disappointment causes pain that is particularly difficult to overcome.

Along the way, we also fail to meet our needs because we hesitate to ask. Some fear to ask because they think that when they receive, they will not have deserved it; they will only have succeeded in putting pressure on the other party. This mostly happens in the workplace where you are afraid to ask for a raise or promotion in fear that your boss will grant it because of the pressure you exert and not because you rightfully deserve it. Others fail to ask because they feel that they are being needy, intrusive, and rude. Introverts particularly worry about how they will make the other party feel if they place their request.

It is also possible to have a list of unmet needs if you do not think of yourself as needing anything. People like these attempt to hide their needs by acting fine while they could be drowning inside.

The fear of rejection and other negative reactions also drives people to suppress their unmet needs. They are frightened of hearing 'no' because it will have an effect on their person.

When you feel insignificant, not good enough, or when you lack a sense of self-worth, you tend to take anything you hear personally. You develop a veil that validates your assumptions and thinking, which is sometimes not objective. The next time you feel frustrated and irritated, retreat and ask yourself one question, "What do I need right now?"

The answer to this question is not often what you are targeting your feelings towards. You could be angry that your husband forgot to buy certain items on your shopping list but really, it is only that you have attached meaning to him buying every item on the shopping list. It could be that him purchasing everything you need shows you that he cares and when he forgets, you assume that his attention is diverted to something else. Although you will still need the groceries, analyzing his forgetfulness through the lens of unmet needs will help you take note of the unmet needs, communicate about it, and work towards a solution.

- Make Peace with the past Unmet Demands

The demands of our pasts are not similar to the demands of the present or the future. While you can act on the present and the future, it is almost impossible to meet a past need today. When it comes to needs like these, instead of agonizing over the indelible pain it has caused, people are better off making peace with the past unmet needs and moving forward. People say that the past is only good for two things: to enjoy the benefits and to learn from it. If a memory does not bring any good feeling, it is best to make peace with it.

The mind is naturally conditioned to remember the past, which makes making peace with painful memories quite difficult. We stay attached to profound experiences and the accompanying emotions both consciously and unconsciously. This makes us prone to reliving them time and again, which festers wounds that add no value to the present life. However, when you consciously and decisively work towards making peace with the past, you experience freedom allows you to forgive others or yourself, move forward, and live up to your potential.

This process can be done in the following steps:

o *Look back on all those past events, however painful*. Letting go does not just involve packing the bags and putting the past behind you. The harder you try to shove your past, the harder it clings to you. Instead, relive the moments, grieve the pain from the unmet needs, the fear and the anxiety you suffered. Although this will be difficult, you will note considerable change and improvement. It may help to write down all those experiences you have kept away from or repressed. Finally, you have exposed the truth!

o *Take in the past*: When you take in the past, you recognize the event and accept it. You do not say, "I wish my mother took time to raise me instead of going out all the time." Instead, you say, "I accept that my mother did not take time to raise me."

I lost my father to cancer at a young age. It took me many years to accept his death. When I finally did, I accepted that I would have to grow up with one parent, and I was okay with it. I must warn you that comparing yourself to others will slow the process of accepting your unmet needs. Had I compared myself to my friends, who were raised in two-parent homes, I would probably still be angry and grieving many years later. Accepting your past means moving on while the gaps are still in it.

- *Look for the sparks*: Just as each cloud has a silver lining, there is good in every experience, however dark. It is difficult to see this at first, but when you become friends with your past, the cards will begin to fall in the right places and you will see the hidden treasure. In my case, I got to have a new relationship with my mom, and this would not have happened otherwise. I became stronger. I was able to comfort others who lost their parents and I now know the importance of a father. I would not dare deny my kids one. What I am saying is that had it not been for your pain, you would not be the awesome person you have become.

- *Stop blaming others*: Trying to change what has already happened is impossible. For lack of a better term, you would be crying over spilled milk. What holds back many people are the limiting beliefs they have about their past, talking about what others should or should not have done. For example, saying "My boss should not have fired me while I was pregnant" or "My mother should have kept me instead of giving me up for adoption" is not going to make you feel better. The event already happened, and as you know, history does not change.

  Instead, try putting yourself in their shoes perhaps, and you will find a different explanation for what happened. For example, you could say, "My mother was financially, psychologically, and emotionally ill-equipped to take care of a baby on her own and bringing me up in this kind of environment would have been unhealthy and unfair to me." When you change how you think about it, you will be able to move on.

- *Do not seek confessions from the guilty party*: We believe that hearing a confession and acknowledgment of guilt from the offender gives closure but sometimes, this is false. Not every person will apologize; some are glad that you are suffering. In fact, no one will intentionally hurt you then do you good. This admission and recognition you seek is only an illusion because until you have dealt with your emotions yourself, you are not off the hook.

- *Forgive forget*: Forgiving is critical in making peace. It rids you off the negativity and judgment. You forgive for your benefit and not the offenders'.

- *Take caution*: Be alert and look out for negative feelings and thoughts that may arise. If they come, let them but do not suppress or give them room. Let them pass. Each thought will tell you how you are progressing. Soon, peaceful thoughts replace painful ones.

- *Consciously let go of your past*: The last step involves your will. You consciously let go and resolve to not let your past dictate your future. Let go for real, knowing that you deserve the best. If you feel that you need therapy at this point, go for it!

- The Psychology of Forgiving Your Past

For a long time, scientists have puzzled at the concept of forgiving and forgetting, and its influence on psychology. They realized that once a victim forgives her transgressor, she is better placed to intentionally forget words and emotions linked to the offense. Those that are unable to forgive have trouble forgetting unwanted memories. Surprisingly, they link forgetting to the very act of forgiving, not just the potential to accept other people's mistakes.

Psychology studies have also found that people with higher forgiveness levels enjoy better health and report lesser cases of anxiety, depression, and anger. Even in intimate relationships with a history of betrayal, greater forgiveness levels were found to lead to more gratifying relationships. Physiologically, a more forgiving person's white blood cell count is significantly lower than that of a grudging person. The body produces white blood cells to fend off infections and diseases. These results show that it benefits both the mind and the body to forgive others.

Forgiving shows that you are putting your future in mind. In a study to determine the link between forgiveness and psychological health, scientists found that people who had accumulated much stress over their lifetime presented worse mental health issues. Among those with high scores on forgiveness measures, stress was not a significant factor affecting their mental health. This study proved that forgiveness is surprisingly more powerful than we would presume. It knocks over the link between psychological distress and mental health.

Similar studies conducted to confirm these findings often have the same result. They find that as forgiveness rises among different people, the lesser the stress levels. In turn, lower stress level lead to a good state of mental health.

The results from these studies are not only good for people who find it easy to forgive, but there is also good news for those who hold grudges. They show that forgiving can be learned, but will need a bit of practice. You will not have to achieve the highest level of forgiveness in the first attempt, but with time, you will realize that the negative emotions no longer exist. It will shed off some of your stress, and ultimately make you feel better.

Start by making effort to develop empathy. Expressive writing and journaling aimed at helping you become more empathetic will be a good place to start. In your writing, be in the shoes of those that offended you and seek to write in an empathetic tone. If you are religious, prayer helps greatly. People who pray for others are less likely to hold grudges and scheme retaliation against them. Only give the process time, do not just give up after the first attempt. Keep trying; persistence breaks all resistance.

- Detect as the Source of Anger Arises

You can detect anger as it comes up because it does not just flare up without warning signs. Anger being a typical physical response, your body prepares for it. These preparations are the tell signs that you are about to explode. Taking precautionary moves and understanding your personal anger traits helps you to get ready and take action before it spirals out of control.

The signs of anger include a sudden headache, pounding heart, faster breathing, clenched jaws and fists, a sudden flash, pacing about, tension in the shoulders and having trouble seeing.

We often think that what others do to us is what leads us to anger. However, anger is more about your interpretation of an event than it is about how you have been treated. Anger, in this case, is fuelled by placing blame, making assumptions, overly critical, obsessing on what others should have done right, and overgeneralizing. Once you are aware that you are doing any of these, quickly distract that thought pattern and focus on another important issue.

Some places, people, and situations could also provoke you to anger. However, pressure and stress are no excuse for anger. You must be in control of your surroundings and avoid unnecessary provocations. In your daily routine, identify people, places, times, and situations that make you upset and unhappy, then come up with ways to avoid them.

Below are a number of anger triggers based on the environment:

o *At the workplace*

- Having a lower salary than a colleague as qualified as you.
- The sight of a bootlicker who gets ahead by crude methods rather than performance.
- The very sight of your employer.
- Knowing more than the supervisor.
- An unkept promise particularly related to salary increment and promotion.
- Being asked to do something you believe to be wrong or unethical.
- Micromanagement by your supervisor.
- Very high expectations that are impossible to live up to.
- Lack of proper compensation for the work you do.
- Criticism from the boss or the client for no good reason.
- A partner being late for an important meeting.
- Verbal attacks and intimidation.
- Sexual harassment.
- Sexism

- Racial profiling and discrimination.
- Disrespect
- Rejection
- Rude customers.

- *At home*

  - Disrespect from a partner or a child, and vice versa.
  - Lack of appreciation from those you care for.
  - Lack of provisions like groceries and money.
  - Domestic violence.
  - Sexual harassment and abuse.
  - A partner or a child being constantly late.
  - Attitude problems.
  - Wrong assumptions and beliefs.
  - Self-judgment
  - Rejection
  - Sexism
  - Unfair division of labor.
  - Mistrust and unfaithfulness.
  - Religious misunderstanding.
  - Misplaced anger.
  - A selfish and inconsiderate person.
  - Belittlement
  - A feeling of low energy.

- *At school (for a child with anger issues)*

  - Unfair treatment by both teachers and students.
  - Racial profiling.
  - Low grades.
  - Homework overload.
  - Disorders like ADHD and IED (Intermittent Explosive Disorder).

- Neglect and trauma.
- Sensory processing problems (trouble processing information).
- Autism
- Undiagnosed and untreated learning issues.
- Comparison with other students.
- Disrespectful acts and remarks.

Chapter 3: Take Control of Your Anger Today

You have both the capability and responsibility for controlling your anger. Anger is a natural emotion, but lack of control could make life quite difficult. Each day, there are sources of anger all around you; there will be traffic snarl-ups, a carefree driver, a careless comment, or the very sight of your boss that makes bouts of anger throb at your temples. While you may have a justifiable reason for your anger, you can choose not to have a negative response by opting to do something else; take control of it.

To do this, practice the following:

- Practice to Be in the Moment, Increase Awareness of Your Emotions

    Like me, you have probably found yourself immediately regretting something you said carried away by emotions. I am known to utter some of the most snarky comments in family gatherings driven by unresolved anger over what someone did or said in the past. The shame and guilt that follows for the rest of the event; you would not envy. Everyone looks at me knowingly, as if to say that I am the wet blanket that dampens their mood. Others begin to avoid me, possibly so that I do not air their dirty laundry in public. The truth is that we all fly off the handle sometimes, and could use help managing our emotions by increasingly becoming aware of them.

    With good reason, contemporary psychology is emphasizing the importance of emotional intelligence. This concept is associated with an improved work performance, more satisfaction in relationships, and an enhanced ability to handle stress. By definition, emotional intelligence is the ability to control and to be aware of your emotions and developing empathy for others. Once you are aware of your emotions and those of others, you are able to run relationships more effectively and be in control when conflicts come up.

Emotional awareness is founded on self-awareness. You get a grip of your emotions when you gain a deep understanding of who you are and how you come off to others. You are able to understand your feelings any time and can identify their source. You are also able to identify physical manifestations of anger such as a sudden headache, an increased heartbeat, or sweaty palms and are able to act on your emotions immediately.

Increasing your level of self-awareness is simple. Begin by taking some time off to study you. Yes, you will study you. Take some time to carefully monitor your emotions. Give an honest answer to questions like "How do I feel now? What causes me to feel this way? How is my body manifesting this feeling?" Once you identified the emotion that you are feeling, label it. Is it anger, anxiety, or fear? Write this feeling down along with what you think could have triggered it. Once this information is on paper, it is now easier to identify what you are dealing with, and you can begin to strategize on what to do to overcome the negative emotion.

Once you are aware of what triggers you and have a response strategy in place, it is time to keep alert in case some emotion pops up. This is what we call mindfulness, or 'being in the moment'. It is simply being very alert to listen to what your feelings and emotions could be whispering to you at any moment. You consciously and actively pay attention to the happenings of the present. When you live in the moment, you realize that you are only an observer of your thoughts and that they do not make you. You only let them slide without suppressing any. It allows your inner being to awaken and experience life, instead of simply going by it.

Developing this awareness holds a number of benefits for you. It will reduce stress, lower pain levels, improve immunity, lower blood pressure, and help you cope with terminal illnesses and the pain from past unmet needs. Once you able to spend time enjoying the moment, you also reduce your susceptibility to heart illnesses. Your body and your mind will begin to feel like happy places for your soul to reside.

When people are mindful, their lives improve significantly. They become more happy, empathetic, and secure. Their self-esteem soars and is more accommodating of their shortcomings. Negative coping behavior, reactivity, and impulsivities like binge eating, attention problems, and depression begin to come down. There is also less fighting in relationships because the people become less defensive and more accepting. It becomes easy to let go when verbally attacked because they realize that not all battles are worth fighting. For these reasons, mindful people have better relationships with others.

As you work and focus on being mindful, do not do it just for the benefits. When you do something expecting results, your focus your mind on the future, and this beats the entire concept of living in the moment. Instead, do it step-by-step knowing that benefits will set in whenever. For now, focus on knowing you.

- Stop and Think Before You Speak/Act

Baby Sleep

When you are angry, you talk intending to communicate something, but most importantly, to express how something has made you feel. However, when emotions are running high, it is easy to let out a careless statement without thinking about it. You only realize that you said something hurtful and damaging moments later. Statements spoken without much thought achieve the opposite; you want to be heard and instead, you drive people away. Aggression is an enemy to intelligent communication. Therefore, there is a need to interrupt the link between emotions and communication by creating room for a thought process.

Many people find it difficult to think before they speak. You might also occasionally suffer the same problem, particularly in instances when you want to prove to everyone the smart person you believe you are. Just to see where you lie, let's conduct a little test.

Assume you are working on a project that you must submit in two hours and your husband or wife rushes into the room. He or she has been watching television and come across an upcoming story about a politician, let's say, Donald Trump. Apparently, the President tweeted something controversial and it has now gone viral. There is a backlash from the people and the conversation surrounding the issue has been heating up. You already know all that because you were scrolling through your Twitter feed a few minutes before. However, your spouse wants to narrate all the nagging details, from what the president said to what the people said.

Do you wait until your spouse has finished narrating, listening keenly, and then let him know that you had come across something similar on Twitter or do you cut their statement short and alert them on your upcoming deadline? If you will sincerely take the first option, you're good to go. If you're like most of us who will succumb to pressure and take the second option, well, we have a lot to learn.

It is not difficult to let people know that you are smart or are already informed of what is happening. First, take a minute before you speak and ask yourself, "Is anything I will say helpful to the situation? Will it make it better or worse?"

If the answer is negative, move on to the next step where you say, "Thank you for telling me that honey. I actually came across something similar on Twitter." Now, try exercising this level of control in a different situation, making sure to use a person you are used to, like a best friend, and if you pass, you are on the right track.

The minute you allow anger to get between you and reason, you end up looking unwise rather than wise. You are forced to make apologies that can be quite embarrassing. The results of speaking or acting without thinking are not as subtle as we have portrayed; it's just hurting another's feelings and getting away with an apology later. This attitude can cause you to lose your job, break the relationship you have with your children, reputation damage, get you arrested, and other unfavorable life-changing events that can shatter your life.

- Take a Chill Pill (Keeping Your Cool)

Assuming that your speech has been thoughtful, and you have not lashed out at anyone, do not allow the negative emotions to flare up again. You probably still feel like chocking someone, smashing them in the face, or running out of the room, but here's what you should do; take a chill pill. If you have already brought rationality into the picture, allow it to direct the course of what you do next. In the meantime, relax. Keep your cool.

Here are a few steps you can take to help you remain calm:

1. Speak to yourself, convincing your person to calm down. Repeat this and any other gentle phrases like 'you're still fine,' 'it will be okay' or 'nothing will change' and any other phrases you find soothing.
2. Leave the heated environment and go elsewhere. Take a walk, ask for a timeout, or go for a run. Do not come back yet; give it some time.
3. While you are out, visualize things that would calm you down like standing beside the ocean, having a massage, or any other soothing activity.
4. If you feel pressed to do something violent or harmful, start counting from 1 to 20, 50 or 100, until the feeling passes. This mentally breaks the link between emotion and acting.
5. Use some cold water to wash your hands and face.
6. Slow down on everything and concentrate on your breathing. Breathing consciously involves slow deep breaths that go in through the nose and out through the mouth.
7. Call a friend or a family member you can talk to about the situation
8. Start replacing the negative thoughts you had previously with positive and rational thoughts, and voila! You are calm now. When angry thoughts try to make their way again, remind yourself that becoming angry will not fix a thing.

- Preventing Anger Issues in the Future

You have already won your first battle with anger in a long time and are wondering, what of the next time? Will I successfully deal with strong negative emotions again? What shall I do in the event I do not have a series of steps to follow then? My answer to this is preparation. Prepare now for future encounters. You are likely to succeed when you are prepared than when you are not.

Start by taking time for yourself and use it to release stress. Take up a hobby or an activity for which doing it makes you happy. You could go swimming, chat with your friends, reading a book, or any other that relaxes you and makes you feel good. If you lean towards reading or being with your friends, kindly combine that with a physically involving activity like going to the gym, swimming, or playing a sport because exercise quickly clears the mind too thereby relieving stress.

Some people adopt and practice relaxation techniques like listening to music, yoga, and meditation. Others start journaling their feelings by recording the experience they had, the factors that triggered the anger, and a description of their response. They also record the thoughts that ran through their mind at the time. Keeping a journal and recording these details will help you reflect on your anger management techniques and to establish any pattern there could be.

It also helps to think of all possible outcomes of an outburst. I did this a few months ago when I flipped out on a friend and slapped him. The slap did not offer much relief. It dawned on me that my next move would hurt him badly or land me in the hands of the law and turned away immediately. The next day, while scrolling through YouTube videos, I found prison documentaries in which prisoners are asked to tell their stories.

The common denominator in all the stories I hear was that a moment's anger had driven the person to act irrationally. It does not take much to have you behind bars; flared up anger, an irrational thought, and there goes your freedom. This thought has carried me over the last few months and not in a single instance have I acted irrationally.

In the same way, take a moment to ponder on your anger moments. What could they cost you? Your freedom? A relationship with your children? A happy marriage with your awesome husband or wife? Your career? Traumatizing your children? What are you ready to exchange for a moment's 'satisfaction'? When you reflect on these things, you are likely to find that getting angry is not worth it. Take note of the emotions that lead you to anger, and those that you feel when you are angry. Is it confusion, depression, anxiety, or frustration? Take note of this feeling and address it appropriately.

Learn how to communicate well with others, even if it means taking a book from the shelf to learn communication skills or watching those you admire handle stressful situations. Do they speak calmly and rational? Try doing what they do. You will realize so much progress. If you prefer learning in a formal set up, go ahead and register for that class. If you need professional help, go ahead and seek counseling. You are in charge of your boat.

- Looking at the Big Picture

A different way to overcome anger is to focus on other things and not your problems. This is what we call looking for the big picture in a situation. It requires you to explore the good aspects of a situation or a person rather than on the small issue that is bringing negative emotions. For example, if you are angry that your spouse forgot to buy some groceries, consider the fact that he or she honored your request and went to the store. Consider also that the spouse bought some of the items on your list. This is worth appreciation. Let him know that you are grateful.

You could also be stressing over your health. An upset stomach or the flu could be causing you to feel frustrated, helpless, and a tad annoyed. However, you are alive and well, you are not lying on a hospital bed, and you get to have people show their love as they take care of you. You have a lot going for you other than the pain you feel.

This is the bigger picture. It puts into focus the positive things about life ignoring the little specs that bring pain and anger. It helps you develop an attitude of gratitude so that during tough times, not necessarily the angry moments, you can focus on what is going well in your life and realize that many of these problems are molehills and not mountains.

The bigger picture need not rotate around you and your affairs. You can sit down and focus on the offender's circumstances. Take into account the unique challenges the person has had to face in life and take note of possible past unmet needs. It is likely that the person is only reacting to his unique challenges. More than blaming, a person like this will need empathy, and you can try giving it to them, mentally, at least. When you think in this direction, you are sure to feel much better and your anger will neutralize. You will find yourself adapting to this mode of thinking and you will easily control your anger. People will begin looking up to you just as you admire other people around you.

Baby Sleep

- Switch Your Perspective

    Interesting fact — human beings are the only creation that gets to choose how it perceives the world around them. You have the freedom to choose your response to the circumstances of life, and how to perceive what happens to you. If a coworker brushes past you causing you to drop a pile of books, you decide whether she did it on purpose or not, independent of her intentions. However you take it, what you perceive stays in your mind and your heart, and influences your emotions.

    Influenced by past unmet needs, most people react based on their old scars and hurt. People with rage, for example, only hear and react to their anger. They see themselves as targets and will use others as targets of their anger too. These people experience selective amnesia at the peak of their anger and when they calm down, many of them cannot even tell what threw them into that rage. They cannot remember what they spoke or did and are often shocked by the violence and harm they cause. Once the incidence has passed, the person is very remorseful.

    Without understanding the nature of people with that kind of rage, it may be impossible to separate the person from his actions. Done repeatedly, you would not be blamed for thinking that the person is taking you for a ride. The idea of amnesia in itself makes it less believable. However, once you learn about what the person is going through, you are less likely to get angry after the feat. You could actually begin to explain to him what happens when he becomes extremely angry, and the person will be prompted to seek help. Alternatively, you could become resentful of them and walk away from such a person. It all depends on what you see.

When dealing with a person prone to anger, whether extreme or mild, you get to make the choice between staying with them, understanding them, or letting them go. However, before you make any permanent decision, consider practicing this exercise.

Begin by reminding yourself of an encounter with the person that left you angry, frustrated, and irritated. Do you remember what the person did to provoke these feelings? Why did the person react as he did? Now, try to come up with two plausible explanations for his actions. Think about how each of the explanations makes you feel. Which of the two makes you feel less angry? Pick that one and frame your mind around this idea. Let this be the reason why the person did that. The method is meant to pick the explanation that will produce the least emotional distress.

Looking at another case, imagine a scenario where you call someone to babysit your children as you run off to work. She is running late and so are you, for your job. You realize that your anger is flaring as you clench your fists and pace around the house. Your first assumption could be that the babysitter is taking advantage of you and wants you to pay her for the time they have not worked. A second assumption could be that the babysitter is caught up in traffic or ran into car trouble and is afraid to call you knowing that she has disappointed you.

If you take the first assumption, you will be fuming mad once she arrives and arguing with her could spoil the day for both of you. If you take the second option, you are likely to remain calm, take the apology when she offers it and heads off to work cheerfully. Take the second option; it will produce the least adverse effects.

Now, apply this reasoning in the situation currently aggravating you and you will be calmer about it.

- Be Assertive (Honest and Polite at the Same Time)

We have discussed techniques and strategies you can take up to work out anger on your end but this does not mean that you should chicken out and take all the blame. Some angry people are wrong and still need to be corrected. As we said earlier, anger is also a genuine feeling that should not be suppressed and should be expressed to indicate your dissatisfaction with the situation as is. Instead of locking your feelings in, consider becoming assertive in your approach.

Assertiveness is a primary skill in communication. When a person is assertive, he stands up for himself and expresses his opinion truthfully without getting angry. Assertiveness is about expressing your thoughts while maintaining control of your feelings, without letting emotions run high. Communicating this way is more effective than talking while exhibiting all kinds of igneous behavior. It is also the most effective way of ensuring a balanced posture so that everyone gets his or her side heard and the issues resolved.

When you are displeased with how something is running or how someone is speaking and treating you, it is wiser to try communicating with them about how you are feeling. It is likely that the person is unaware of how it is affecting you. Being assertive, you will be able to express yourself properly and check your emotions intelligently. You will listen and possibly say, "I get what you are saying but if you consider the issue from my point of view, you will see that..."

Assertiveness does not mean that you should be sacked into the individual's emotions; only agree with them if it makes sense to you. Otherwise, stick to your opinion and maintain your position. You are only required to tolerate a different opinion and not to compromise.

It may take a while to develop this skill, but the more you consciously choose to be assertive when dealing with anger, the more the skills will increasingly be engrained in you. It will become a part of your character and you can confidently express your opinion even in heated discussions, without engaging in childish screaming and whining. More importantly, it will earn you respect among your peers.

- Adopt a Type-B Personality

The differences in our personalities also play a role in how we deal with heavy situations. Type-A persons are competitive, highly stressed, addicted to achievements, and conscious of their status. They love to multi-task, are constantly trying to achieve a goal, are constantly on edge, and are prone to heart conditions and diseases. Type-B personalities are relaxed, laid-back, recognize the social aspect of life, and are able to prioritize. Type-B personalities like to work with others on projects to avoid overburdening themselves, believing that the way to achieve happiness in life is to balance out everything.

The highly tense inside environment that a Type-A personality has already created makes them quite irritable. They are advised to strive to adopt a number of Type-B tendencies such as:

  o *A wider view*: Type-A personalities think in one direction, and one direction only. Their minds focus on work. Type-

B personalities, on the other hand, express interest in a number of things beyond their work such as hobbies, spirituality, patriotism, chatting with family and friends, relationships, and nature. Adopting this worldview could help Type-A personalities ease the pressure they put on work and achievement.

- *Relaxing*: Type-A personalities are famous for their sense of agency. Being one, I am always dragging people all over in fear of being late. This person likes to keep time and can be tipped off by lateness, even by minutes. Type-Bs enjoy the flexibility and do not worry about the tasks they will not have accomplished by the end of the day. Taking up this trait could significantly ease the anxiety Type-As feel in traffic jams during rush hour.

- *Considering others not just yourself*: Type-As are not selfish, but they tend to capitalize 'I' in all they do. They hold themselves in high regard and are constantly speaking about their achievements. Type-As are likely to think that all negative comments are directed to them, and will react fast. Type-Bs are humble and do not feel entitled. They are likely to let a negative comment go by even when directed at them. This humble nature would go a long way in helping Type-As lower their ego and irritability.

- *Avoiding competition*: Type-As have numbers on their fingertips, ready to count to you their achievements. It would be easier and more socially accommodating to say, "The year has been productive" instead of running numbers on the number of deals you were a part of. You are more likely to be unhappy and embarrassed when Type-Bs fail to acknowledge these achievements. Instead of focusing on the achievement, Type-As should learn to enjoy the process and the experience.

- *Inquisitive*: Type-B personalities are constantly running around looking to enlarge their horizon in the form of diverse relationships, listening to different viewpoints and life experiences. Type-As should seek to explore life to increase their scope. They should also get to experience the thrills of uncertainty over which Type-Bs thrive.

To that end, Type-As are encouraged to expand their world to reduce the stress they accumulate focusing on one thing only.

Chapter 4: Self-Management for Better Mental Health

Taking steps towards caring for your mental health does not always involve meds and therapy. At its basic, you can also care for your mental wellness by identifying what you desire or need, however small, and then go ahead to meet those needs. It can be as easy as taking a glass of water to go out with friends or going for a run, anything to make your mind relax.

As the world gets busier, you can easily be caught up in beating deadlines at work or meeting the needs of your family that you forget about yourself and your health. Moms and single dads are particularly prone to this. They manage a career, care for the family, and barely get time to themselves. Although they develop resilience as they go, one can easily crack under this mountain of pressure. In a country where one in every four is now suffering from mental health problems, it is time you took your place and care for your mental health.

Below are a number of points that will guide your journey of self-care:

- Stress Management

    Stress is a natural part of life and although some stressors are easy to avoid, such as having a long-distance relationship or joining a sports team, others are difficult to avoid. You only have to find a healthy way to respond to them, beginning from an individual level.

    Prevention should be your first action plan to cut short the buildup of stressors. Begin by taking good care of yourself emotionally, mentally, and physically by feeding properly, exercising, taking some time to relax, and getting an adequate amount of sleep. Instead of having to check numerous items on your list daily, choose to do less to have relaxation time. Prioritize your activities by examining what is of most importance to you today, and in the next 5 years. Set limits to what you can do by turning down some people with a simple 'no' to avoid overworking yourself. It is also important to enjoy the fruits of what you do by setting aside some time and money for fun activities with friends and family.

After blocking the additional stressors' path, focus on relieving the existing stress. Examine what you like to do to take off some pressure. Some people prefer to eat or drink their feelings sitting with a bottle of beer, eating fast foods, or drowning their tears in a bucket of ice cream. While these methods may be effective, how about trying out healthier options like seeking help from a professional or a friend, writing your feelings, changing the environment, or gaming. You could also adopt relaxation techniques like yoga, breathing, and meditation.

If your schedule or the nature of your environment does not allow you to do and the activities listed above, you may need a complete behavior change. Changing how you are and what you do will need considerable effort on your side. However, if you are still intent on following through, start by turning these activities into goals. For example, you can dedicate three hours each week to chat and catch up with friends. You could also set aside ten minutes each day to focus on breathing. These goals should be put down on paper to increase the chance of following them through. Remember to reward positive steps and to ask for help where needed.

- Achieve the Balanced Life

The boundaries between work and a personal life continually thin out, and work could be limiting your personal life. Creating a clear demarcation can be quite difficult especially if your career is quite demanding or that you anticipate changes like layoffs at your place of work. In addition, technology has merged work and home life, creating an instant connection between the two. However, establishing a healthy balance between the two is not impossible; you could apply some strategies to help you restore that balance.

Before we evaluate the process of establishing and reestablishing a work-life balance, it is prudent for us to evaluate what awaits you if you do not take action. A poor work-life relationship will have detrimental effects on you. First, you will end up fatigued and when tired, your productivity automatically lowers negatively affecting your reputation and the chances of you holding that job much longer.

Secondly, there is a chance that you could stretch yourself into poor health. Too much pressure on your body from accumulated stress will, in turn, affect your immune system, making you susceptible to all kinds of diseases. Come to think of it, if you are working, when was the last time you saw the sun and basked in its vitamin D? Do you get time to prepare healthy meals at home? Certainly not.

Thirdly, you lose time that you could have spent bonding with family and friends. If you are constantly working, it is likely that you will miss important milestones and events in the lives of your loved ones. This may harm these relationships and cause you to lose them eventually. Losing these relationships will cause you much pain, sorrow, and regret.

Lastly, the more you give yourself, the more people will expect from you. If you work for more hours, you will be very productive and given more responsibilities that will only make your life more stressful.

To strike a balance between these two important spheres of life, you will need two winning strategies:

o The first is to set limits. Understand that without limits, your obligations will take all your time, without leaving any for a social life. Set limits by doing the following:

1. *Say no sometimes.* No is not disrespectful, it only sets boundaries between what you can and cannot do. It stops you from taking on too much responsibility and gives you time to do what is meaningful to you.
2. *Manage your time more efficiently.* Setting aside time for an activity reduces the frequency of interruptions and prevents one activity from dragging for too long. In addition, you could avoid or delegate the activities that are difficult and those that are draining to focus on tasks that interest you. Only do what is necessary for that day.
3. *Weigh your options.* If you get the opportunity to work flexible hours, work from home, or schedule your hours, take advantage of it. When you have control over when you work, you will be less stressed about it.
4. *Reduce interruptions and shorten the concentration span.* The average person will maintain maximum concentrations for 90 minutes at a time. After that, the level of attention decreases significantly. Interruptions increase the time it takes to finish a task, which means that one task can drag on for a long time thereby creating boredom.

5. *Check your email less often.* The more you check your emails throughout the day, the more you will be distracted from your duties. It will keep you wondering, and you will even try to help others instead of focusing on your own roles.
6. *Have a plan.* A plan lists the things that need to be done and allocates adequate time for each. Have a plan that takes into consideration both phases of life to avoid one phase of your life taking over your entire calendar. Stick to the plan and avoid getting sucked into other people's plans.

- The second strategy for keeping a healthy work-life balance is to begin to take care of yourself better. When you maintain a healthy lifestyle, you are able to cope with stress better. A healthy lifestyle will require you to sleep adequately, eat healthy foods, and set aside some time for relaxation and fun. A support system in the form of family and friends is also essential because they cover you in times of need and crises. Some will also help with daily tasks so that you do not have to do everything yourself.

While it is possible to re-strategize and re-organize your life on your own, it helps to seek professional counsel sometimes. For example, everything may look equally important to you and you may be unable to set priorities. However, a professional will be able to look at each activity objectively and help you gain perspective on what to do. You may be prioritizing taking your child to see the dentist at the expense of a board meeting or prioritizing a board meeting instead of attending your child's first football game. You could have your spouse take your child to the dentist while you make effort to be present during one of your child's most significant events such as his first game. You only need to determine what is of most importance at a time, and a professional could help you weigh each option.

Striking a healthy balance in life is a process and not a one-day event. It goes on for the rest of your life but changes as your interests, your work, and your family life changes. You only need to examine what you prioritize occasionally and to make the right adjustments.

Why Is a Good Sleep Important for Anger Management?

Sleep on it. Many of us have heard this advice more times than we can count. It does not make sense when you think about it keenly. How are you to make a decision while asleep? Turns out that this is not one of the old wives tales, sleeping does indeed help to make better decisions. Research shows that sleep influences retention, emotions, decision-making, mood, and anger, among others.

While you sleep, your mind and body are fast at work. The body takes the opportunity to clear toxins, take out wastes, balance hormones, and repair tissues. This process is complex and requires adequate time to complete. Therefore, when interrupted, it interferes with your temperament, memory, emotional regulation, and response.

When your mood and emotions are right, you are likely to take time to assess the situation deeper and to give a reasonable response. You probably heard a parent say that their child who was throwing a tantrum needed a nap to calm down. This is true because sleeping will help the mind re-evaluate its emotional processing of the situation at hand.

Your memory is key to your decision-making ability because you rely on the past or what you have learned to weigh out merits and demerits. Sleep determines how memories are stored and retrieved in the brain. It also influences the accuracy with which you remember events.

Therefore, when you sleep adequately, you are likely to make good decisions and to be happy with the results.

Researchers say that sleep-deprived people tend to make unethical decisions. Sleepy people at work are likely to be sloppy and inefficient, behave defiantly, be rude to others, and intentionally reduce their productivity. This is thought to be largely because the lack of sleep deprives them of the ability to control themselves. It is also thought that glucose levels at the frontal lobe could be depleted, affecting the ability to make decisions and think complex thoughts.

All these factors make a strong case for why you need to value your hours of sleep. A regular sleeping schedule, proper nutrition, exercise, and taking time off are all you need to function optimally. You will enjoy a balanced emotional state that will help you make good decisions and maintain healthy relationships.

If you encounter an emotionally charged situation, take some time to rest. You only need to clear your mind actively with some meditation or breathing to avoid the events of the day tempering with your rest. When you wake up, you will have a changed attitude and perspective.

Best Routines and Tips for Better Sleep

It is difficult to get a good night's sleep while you are still tossing at 3 AM in the morning. Many people become weary in the evening anticipating the agony they will have in the night as they helplessly try to catch some sleep. Some result to medication to ease the process. The truth is that you are not as helpless as you may think. You determine the quality of sleep you get. Just like how the feeling you have when you wake up determines the quality of your day, so do the activities of the day determine the quality of sleep you get.

When you go looking into information about sleep and sleep habits, it is likely that you will find many sources advocating for 'sleep hygiene'. This term is used to refer to the healthy sleeping habits that are meant to help you fall asleep undistracted. These habits are recommended for the treatment of persons suffering from prolonged insomnia during cognitive behavioral therapy. Sleep hygiene enables you to relax and gain control over thoughts that traditionally prevent you from sleeping well.

Below is a description of the practices and techniques to help you achieve sleep hygiene.

- Align Yourself with Your Body's Sleep and Waking up Cycle

  Keeping up with the body's natural sleep and waking up cycle helps you sleep better. If you stick to a regular schedule, you will feel more bouts of energy and refreshment compared to when you sleep intermittently. Begin by setting and sticking to a regular sleep and waking up schedule daily. This helps the body to set its internal clock and readjust itself to enhance the quality of sleep. Choose a time when you are the most tired in order to cut out the tossing and turning. If the schedule allows you enough sleeping time, you should be awake even without an alarm. If you find yourself still needing the alarm, try sleeping earlier.

  Do not allow yourself to get drowsy after a meal. If you feel sleep setting in, do something distracting like cleaning dishes to avoid sleeping before bedtime and having to wake up later in the night. You may also want to limit your napping during the day. Napping may make sleeping at night increasingly difficult. However, if you really need one, limit it to 15-20 minutes only early in the afternoon. In addition, avoid sleeping in during the weekends because when sleeping schedules clash, your symptoms may get worse. Instead, opt for a nap during the day.

- Watch Your Food

Just as you expected, your meals determine how you sleep, particularly those taken just before bedtime. You must have had to stay up sometime because of an upset stomach or discomfort. When you eat, avoid heavy large meals at night, but eat your dinner early avoiding spicy food that can cause you heartburn in the night. Keep off alcohol because it distracts your sleep cycle. Limit your nicotine and caffeine intake during the day as their effects last even up to twelve hours after consumption. Cut back on refined carbs and sugars also because the energy in them can spring you back to consciousness even in deep sleep. Lastly, avoid drinking too many fluids to reduce bathroom visits in the night.

- Your Sleep Environment Should Matter

Although a bedtime routine allows your body to relax in readiness for sleep, even the slightest environment changes could affect your sleep. Your room needs to be quiet, dark, cool and ventilated. The bed should be comfortable, with clean bedding that allows you to turn and stretch without getting entangled. Maintain silence and when you cannot eliminate noise from outside, use earplugs to avoid distraction. Ensure that you reserve your bed for sex and sleeping only, and keep away all work, study items, and gadgets.

- Silence Your Mind

Make effort to avoid dragging any residual anger, stress, and worry to bed because they keep your brain from unwinding and seeking fresh inspiration.

- Get Back Your Sleep

In the event you wake up in the night and have trouble getting back to sleep, the following tips could help you overcome sleeplessness.

1. *Avoid thinking about it*: If you start stressing the fact that you are unable to sleep, you only influence your brain to stay alert. Instead, breathe and focus on how your body responds. Breathe in slowly and out slowly. Repeat this exercise and feel your body relaxing again.

2. *Focus on relaxation, not sleep*: While you may be trying to sleep, anxiety will only keep you from sleeping. Meditate and visualize your body relaxed and in complete rest. Relaxation is also good since it rejuvenates the body just as sleep does.

3. *Do something quiet and non-stimulating*: If you still cannot sleep, it may be time to get out of your bed and do something worthwhile, at least. Ideally, take a book and read it under dim lights. Avoid screens because they would signal to the brain that it is waking time.

4. *Put it down on paper*: If you roused from your sleep worried about something or a new idea came to your mind, take a paper and pen it down; you will worry about it the next day. Drift back to sleep knowing that a good sleep will charge you to deal with the hustles of the next day.

Transform Your Anger into Constructive Action

Children in pain or frustrated from not having their way lose it sometimes. They roll on the ground, jump up and down, yell and cry their tears out. Parents call it tantrums, a hissy fit, a melt-down and a whole load of names. You may have seen it at home, school, or at the mall. However, as a teenager, a young adult or an adult, you cannot start rolling because you are upset. You are expected to have mastered the art of channeling your anger and fury into constructive activities. Parents teach us from an early age.

Despite the high expectations on an adult, emotions will occasionally overwhelm you. There are new situations and stimuli every day that you are not equipped to deal with. This is the reason many people are still trying to get a hold of anger management techniques. One of the most effective ones is to channel that anger into something else. Anger is a form of energy, and since you cannot destroy energy, you can transform it into something useful just as lightning can be channeled into power.

To channel anger is to direct the energy you feel towards a worthwhile task so that you are able to keep that energy away from your mind and emotions. The task to which you are directing energy should always be positive. Otherwise, you will become destructive, driven by your anger. For example, you can go for a run and do an extra mile, read and respond to countless unread emails, or complete that task that you have postponed time and again. Only ensure that what you engage in is productive.

Some people use channeled anger to make plans. Angry people are determined. They are looking for revenge and they want it now. They demand success. In the spirit of determination, they can turn this rage into a business plan, a savings plan, and any other idea that will benefit them in the future.

I have seen someone turn his anger into a cab business. My friend's father called for a cab to take him to a meeting with investors he believed would change his life instantly. He had dreamt of starting a restaurant but whenever he made steps to execute his idea, everything came tumbling down. He arrived late and the investors were not impressed, especially because he arrived an hour late. Frustrated by the cab driver, my friend's father sat down on a bench in the park and drew a plan for what would be a successful cab business. His anger birthed the career that transformed his life. He does not recall his restaurant ideas. You too can transform an unpleasant experience into an amazing idea that will change your life and change the world.

After drawing up a plan, do not forget to execute it. What is a thought or a plan without execution? As soon as you have a plan down on paper, begin to execute it. Do the things you intended to do while you still have the energy and the will to do them. Take advantage of that wave of determination and begin to catapult yourself to success systematically.

Many people begin to doubt themselves at this stage. They become contemplative and allow the doubts to flood their minds, interrupting the course of action. Some people begin to doubt their abilities while others wonder what people will think. It is the reason many talented writers having manuscripts collecting dust in their drawers. They were afraid to take them for publishing fearing rejection. It is also the reason others have not started their dream business wondering what society will think of them if they become entrepreneurs instead of focusing solely on children. It is also the reason others have not submitted their college application papers. In truth, we all have things we did not do because we allowed our fears and thoughts to get in the way.

To avoid this delay, move now in the spirit of your channeled energy. Do not stop to think, do not second-guess yourself. These days, whenever a thought that could potentially stop me comes, I stop and ask myself, "What worst could happen?" If I submit my manuscript, the worst that could happen is the publishers sending me away. So what? There are other publishing houses.

Begin to ask yourself the same question. What worst could happen if you sent in your application to that college you desire to attend? At best, they will take you. Worst case scenario, they will reject your application. Pat yourself on the back either way. You made an effort.

If you are yet to observe this, allow me to share with you what I have. 9 out of 10 times, people reward effort and not performance. A person can have talent and do nothing about it while another can keep making effort and succeed. It is said that persistence breaks resistance.

Let us try to get this into perspective. Pretend that you are an investor or a sponsor of a kind. Whenever you hesitate to do something because you fear failure, ask yourself, "If I were an investor, who would I invest in? A person who tried to do something once and succeeded immediately or the one that doing something many times before succeeding?"

While succeeding in the first attempt shows ability and competence, making several attempts communicates desire, passion, determination, drive, and a desire to know. You would most certainly pick the second candidate. Therefore, keep trying. Keep making effort to succeed and one day, your efforts shall bear fruit.

Although you may want to implement your strategy very fast, it is still wise to double-check to ensure that there are no mistakes. Sometimes, doing things in a rush can lead to failure. For example, if you plan to open a restaurant, check to confirm you have the right premise. Review also the outlay of your plans to ensure that they are right so that adrenaline does not lead you to do things you wouldn't do.

In conclusion, let anger be the rocket fuel that drives you out of your comfort zone into success realms you never thought you would achieve.

Into Practicing Fitness

Talking of ways to channel built-in rage, how about delving into the world of physical activity? Experts speak of a strong correlation between emotional health and exercise. They recommend it for managing stress, anger, and rage. When you exercise while driven by these strong emotions, you are able to kick harder, run longer, and jump higher than you do when in a peaceful state. Experts recommend running, weight-lifting, boxing, and HIIT.

If the high-energy exercises are not for you, opt for aerobics. Do 3 sets of triceps extensions, bicep curls, and side raises, ten at a time. Focus on the contracting muscles and let your rage be felt there.

If you are down and sad, it is better to exercise as a group. Being around people, even strangers could cheer you up. Group workouts are known to produce endorphins, the feel-good hormone that lifts your spirits. Do anything to return to your cheerful self.

Into a New Hobby

Anger and rage can also be channeled into a hobby. Below are a number of creative hobbies you can take up to calm down.

- Gardening

    After working all day seven or six days a week, it is easy to feel like an alien when you go outside. You lose all connection that you had with the outside world. However, there is a genius way to regain this connection and that is through gardening.

Scientists say that this hobby is perfect for lifting your spirits when you feel stressed and angry.

A study in the Netherlands subjected a group of people to a strenuous and stressful task and on completing asked them to split into two groups, each choosing between gardening and reading to lower their stress levels. At the end of the exercise, subjects who chose gardening were found to be in a better mood than those who chose reading proving that gardening is an effective stress-reliever.

Gardening is made effective not only by the feel of nature as you interact with the soil but also by a bacteria living in the dirt. Evidence shows that the ground hosts a bacterium called *Mycobacterium vaccae* which is known to cheer people up. This harmless bacterium boosts the production of serotonin which enhances the mood. People who are exposed to the bacteria from childhood are also reported to have a healthy immune system when older. It just might be of benefit for you to play in the dirt.

- Painting and Drawing

This is one hobby known to help people overcome their trauma and stress. Therapists use it to treat psychological distress from domestic abuse, emotional trauma, depression, physical abuse, anxiety, and other psychological problems. Prison inmates who draw are said to have a positive mood change that helps them to gain a locus of control. However, even without professional direction, you can reap the benefits of this hobby.

When you sculpture, draw, or paint, your brain produces dopamine that activates the body's reward system. This system is known to increase creativity and lower distractions like stress and self-doubt. Therefore, when you engage in any of these activities, you feel pleasure, ownership, and freedom.

- Photography

Photography is a hobby that anyone can pick up, unlike other creative hobbies that require some talent. You only use a camera lens to capture existing beauty, without having to create anything. The beauty of photography is that it teaches you to see evident beauty and that which is not so evident. Photography changes your worldview. You begin to view things from multiple angles, most of which other people would not see. You also get to notice what you would overlook normally.

The effect of seeing beauty in everything is that you become happier, fulfilled, and satisfied. However, there is a learning curve involved.

Chapter 5: Tips to Handle a Partner with Anger Issues

While you may know how to manage your anger and channel it to productive causes, these techniques do not work when you are calm and dealing with an angry person. This is a whole other ball game. You will need to remain calm and help them work through their emotions carefully to avoid their contagious negative energy rubbing up on you.

Dealing with an angry partner is particularly difficult because it involves a combination of volatile emotions like love, anger, jealousy, and frustration among others that erupts fast. It is also a challenge because if the anger bursts are occasional, you may find yourself resenting the person or developing another character that is not you. You may also be tempted to change them, which often works against you.

Here's how to deal with an angry partner without going nuts!

Maintain Your Cool

When your partner is lashing at you and possibly making unfounded statements, the one thing you want to do is to lash back at them, defend yourself, and expose them for the liars they truly are. This is not a wise thing to do. When you consciously choose to remain calm, your partner will get over his or her emotions quicker and then you can reason out together.

Keeping calm is only a strategy to keep things from spilling over, however, it does not eliminate the fact that both of you are angry. It comes from a mature realization that you will not achieve anything if both of you are screaming at each other. The issue at hand should wait until both of you are sober-minded and calm.

Keeping your cool also means that you do not get to sit and mimic their reactions, make faces or acting withdrawn. Either of these will only add heat to an already messy situation because body language communicates as effectively as verbal communication. Instead, nod and only give a brief verbal response where needed. The brief response should be something like, "I hear you" rather than raise your concerns or insulting them saying, "How dumb can you be." Vicious statements like these will only get you into trouble and make it even more difficult for the partner to calm down.

If you do not understand a point the partner is making, respectfully and calmly ask for more details. That way, the person will feel that he or she is heard. In explaining to you their concerns, they may also get a chance to re-evaluate the reason for letting their emotions flare up as such. It helps to remain warm to the side of this person that you like. Focus on that in your mind. Remind yourself that you love him or her and that the anger shall pass.

Identify the Triggers

Anger is birthed by pain and hurt, and when a person is angry, he is only trying to manifest that pain. When a partner is angry at you, it does not automatically mean that you hurt them. People sometimes take out their emotions on the softest and safest target. Not to mean that you are out of the equation; it could be that you opened old wounds of his past unmet needs with something you said or did.

Just to help the men, it could be that the anger your girlfriend is projecting towards you for not buying her a gift is rooted in the fact that you are yet to propose. Ladies are deeply hurt when the man is not showing any signs of commitment, making them question the entire relationship. Or, she could also be hurting from the memories of something that happened to her a long time ago. Or, she may be hurting from something that happened in her personal life like losing a job.

Many times, it is difficult to point directly at the reason a person is angry, which makes keeping calm and listening to them quite sensible. When you listen to them, you are able to filter out the anger trigger under all that mile of emotion. Many times or half the time, the anger will have nothing to do with you or your relationship. It could be from other areas in your partner's life spinning out of control.

Communicate in a Productive Manner

Once both parties calm down, agree on a set time to address the anger and the issues underlying. Be gentle when speaking about the emotions your partner expressed and how they made you feel. This is not meant to help you play victim but to show him or her that the issues also affect you.

Talking about the issues should not provide an opportunity for you to rant and present a list of your partner's failures. If you believe that your partner is lying or has ludicrous ideas, which you possibly already do, do not say it aloud. Allow them to vent out unashamedly because it creates a safe environment for self-expression. This is particularly important for men because many of them fear opening up to talk about their feelings. It also maintains his dignity because he will feel that even the least of his feelings matter to you.

Ask questions to help you understand the situation better and to help your partner connect the dots better. For example, ask "Why does that make you feel…" or "How does that influence this?" In asking these questions, you will realize that you were at fault or your partner will realize that he or she has blown the situation out of proportion. Either way, work towards protecting each party's pride and developing a self-correct attitude for the sake of your relationship.

In case you realize that indeed you contributed to your partner's anger or helped to open old wounds and hurts, apologize sincerely. Even when what you did feels trivial to you, realize that it was significant enough to cause him or her to go off. However, only apologize for what you did because it will be more hurtful if your partner realizes that you only apologized so the issue can rest. Kindly note that you are also responsible for how your partner perceives your actions. If you did something and unintentionally hurt your partner, apologize for that too. However, if you are not responsible for the hurt, do not apologize for it. For example, if your partner misplaced his car keys, say "Sorry that you misplaced your keys" and do not take the blame for it.

Choose Your Battles

You probably heard the phrase 'pick your battles' in a number of settings. This phrase originated from the military in reference to their combat activities. When they picked their battles, they lost some fights, but the mission was to win the war. This simply means that you should not waste your emotional resources, time, or energy engaging in a battle you will certainly not win.

People have and are entitled to their beliefs, preferences, expectations, and opinions, which can make the relationship a battlefield when either side is not willing to bow. Religion and political differences effectively create this kind of environment and it is best to exercise restraint on your part, at least. While you can talk and argue with your partner about anything, it is best to be selective and let go, reserving your energy only for that which fosters peace and matters. If you insist on fighting over everything, you may end up winning the arguments but at the expense of your relationship.

Exercise Patience

Most certainly, resolving the issue at hand will not magically wand off your partner's anger issues. It may take years before your partner is able to overcome the pain, the fear and the helplessness he or she feels. In another instance, your partner will yet again use anger to shield his or her inner feelings and to gain a sense of control. This is the reason it is important to understand the underlying issue so that the occasional outbursts do not make you resentful of them. What will hold you down is your conscious and consistent intentions to work on your relationship and help your partner through the process. Be patient as he or she makes effort to detach from the underlying factors and in due time, your investment will pay.

Empathize

When you have understood what your spouse is going through, you are able to show empathy even if the person is not able to open up and you are sure that something significant is bothering him, making him scared or embarrassed to speak up. Other times, the angry party cannot even tell where the anger is coming from. Whatever the reason, you love your partner and it hurts you when he or she is hurting. Empathize.

Here's how to empathize. First, pray. I have found prayer to be an effective tool towards understanding the pain of others. It gets you to the point of admitting that you are powerless too, and cannot resolve the issue yourself; you need a higher power. It reminds you to view your spouse through a humane lens, realizing that your partner is also prone to mistakes and weaknesses. This attitude will soften your heart and melt any resentment you have towards your spouse. Prayer allows you to ask God for joy, peace, endurance, and the motivation you need to press on.

The second step towards empathy is becoming a safe place for your partner even when he or she does not reciprocate. This step is quite difficult. It demands unconditional love without the assurance of receiving the same in the future. However, if you assure your partner that you can a safe space, he or she will open up. The walls he or she uses to shield and hide will fall and the relationship will transform for the better.

The third step in showing empathy is to be consistent in giving it. Consistency in relationships is key to establishing confidence and trust. If you become a safe space for your partner today, ensure that you do not use his or her weaknesses against them tomorrow. Your partner will have difficulty trusting you in the future and the anger can only get worse because he or she does not have anyone to share with. Of course, there will be days when you are angry and vindictive towards one another, but maintain consistency in presenting love and acceptance.

Empathy will indeed bring the two of you closer and save your relationship.

Be Respectful and Firm

For any relationship to work, boundaries must be set. They govern and clearly demarcate the difference between personal space, personal interests, principles, and values, and that which is shared with a partner. However, just as 'rules are meant to be broken,' your partner, especially one prone to anger, will try to shift them occasionally. Some of the shifts are done unintentionally while in others, the partner intends to test how far he or she can go (I have tried that myself).

Anger should not be an excuse for any reckless behavior. Let your partner know that whichever state he or she is in, your boundaries must be respected. Make a decision on what you can tolerate and what you cannot stand, then bring it to the partner's knowledge. They may insist on shifting the boundary lines, still, be firm about what you mean, but do it respectfully. These boundaries are not born out of selfishness. Instead, they help to cultivate mutual respect.

In the event that a partner crosses a line when he or she flares up, bring it up in the talk you have when he or she calms down. Clearly indicate the boundary your partner crossed, how you felt, and what the consequences of your partner doing so are. For example, if you do not tolerate body shaming, you may say, "I do not appreciate that you spoke about my height in a manner to pull me down or intimidate me. It made me feel small and looked down upon. I am unwilling to be with a person who brings me down every instance he gets, blaming it on the anger."

In this statement, you will have indicated that he crossed the line by speaking negatively about your height, that it made you feel insignificant, and that you are unwilling to tolerate a partner that puts you down whenever he is angry. Saying that you are unwilling to tolerate body shaming does not mean that you will be walking out on the relationship, it gives him the opportunity to shape up or ship out. In all honesty, being in a relationship with someone that makes you feel insignificant and small is unhealthy.

Seek Influence Rather Than Control

Avoid making effort to change your partner. It will get you no results. Instead, seek to influence him by showing him the positives of your position. Just like mentoring, influence is gradual. It shifts your focus from what your partner is doing or thinking wrong and you begin to focus on being on your best behavior so that the partner begins to learn from you.

For example, if your partner lashes out when in anger, avoid lashing out when he makes you angry. Be calm and gentle even where you feel an angry reaction is deserved. It is likely that your partner will notice it and when he gets angry the next time, he will begin to show some level of control in how he expresses his emotion. Slowly, you will begin to win the partner to your side.

There is an expression that suggests that you can catch more flies with honey than vinegar. This expression illustrates the concept of influence over control. Sweetness is able to pull an individual to your side better than beating their head down and dragging them around. Have you heard people say that you are the average of five people you are closest to and that bad company ruins good morals? These phrases revolve around the power of influence. I hear my friends saying control breeds resistance, which could be true. There is an innate desire to go against the grain sometime, and being asked to conform to your partner's ideology might be one.

Therefore, in instances where you desire positive outcomes, lean toward influence. It is gradual but effective.

Do Not Put up with Insulting and Disrespectful Behavior

There is not a reason in the world that sufficiently explains why you should put up with disrespect and bad behavior to maintain a relationship. If your partner treats you with disrespect or by his actions you read that the problem is only escalating, set or strengthen your boundaries. Let your partner know what you can and cannot accept in the relationship and emphasize that you will leave if the boundaries are crossed.

Your boundaries should not deter you from noticing red flags either. Almost all domestic abuse incidences start with a demonstration of anger by either throwing or breaking things, shouting, acting out in public, physical aggression, verbal abuse, and any other sign that potentially frightens you. Once the partner begins to show any of these signs, take precaution and leave the room. In addition, rather than dealing with similar incidences for the rest of your life, consider leaving for good.

Walk Away

It is difficult to be the one that picks the pieces of your relationship repeatedly. Relationships are meant to be two-way and if you are the one that constantly fights for it, it is only right for you to try something different. Some people have a dismissive and condescending attitude, and will not change their minds even when you go to great lengths to influence them positively. Sometimes, the company your partner keeps could be the problem and if you are fighting to influence him against the influence of his five buddies, you are fighting a losing battle.

Walking away is as good for you as it is for him. For example, you shouldn't have to accommodate verbal abuse because it could lead to hurt and abuse that will affect your current and future relationships. Women are particularly good at remembering what someone said. Therefore, if a person insults or body shames you during one of his outbursts, it is likely that you will remember the insult for the rest of your life. A man whose ego is wounded by words or actions will also take time to overcome this hurt if he ever does. This is the reason many people's self-esteem lowers in relationships.

If you feel like the situation will not change, walk away, to save both of you. It will save you from emotional trauma and the possibility of abuse. It will give your partner the opportunity to grow up and learn to respect personal boundaries. Hopefully, your partner will have learned a lesson and behave better in their next relationship. In addition, this loss could push your partner to seek professional help.

Chapter 6: Dealing with Children and Family Members with Anger Issues

Children are little bundles of joy, but as they grow up, this joy can turn into frustration especially if the child has anger issues. It is difficult to know where to begin when handling an angry child. Some children also have a lot of anger pent up in them and will yell and become aggressive at the slightest provocation. Fits like these can leave parents, guardians, caregivers, and teachers wondering what to do.

Angry family members can pose a challenge too when dealing with them. It is possible that you do not know enough about them to come up with an origin for their pain. For example, it is likely that you do not know everything that has happened in your parent's life from birth, and sometimes, even a sibling will surprise you. It is important to learn how to handle their anger and pain, being careful to show respect for their individual life journeys.

A Child with Anger Issues

When dealing with a child, beware that the child is watching you. The manner in which you handle your own or the child's anger sets the precedence for how the child handles anger for the rest of his or her life unless otherwise influenced. It determines how the two of you will handle subsequent disappointments and frustrations. If you do not want to have to deal with tantrums in the future, work on it today.

Here are some tips to help you deal with an angry child.

Set Lower Expectations

When dealing with children, make certain to factor in their ages. A child does not have the knowledge resources you have, the experience you have had, or know how to control emotions like you have learned have and practiced over the years. A child is only now learning about life. The little they know is what you have taught them and what they have been exposed to in their environment around them.

A child also magnifies small things. Their little mind is yet to understand causal links between events. I once watched a child cry uncontrollably because he had dropped a pen and did not know how to get it back from the ground. I thought to myself, "It only takes bending and picking it up," but this child did not know this. He possibly thought that it is the worst thing that could happen in life. When dealing with a child, whether two or ten years old, remember that their understanding is limited. Do not rush the process; let them grow their understanding a little bit at a time.

A child is also said to be the book in which parents and other adults inscribe indelibly their beliefs, values, and morals. Everything that happens to them is a learning process. Do not get angry when your child shouts at you; do not expect him to know that he should respect his elders. Where could he have learned it from anyway? Calm down and explain social values to them and just as it takes practice to know algebra, it will take firm and repeated teaching for the child to conform to your ways.

Validate Emotions

As a parent, guardian, caregiver, or any other adult taking care of a child, it is important to value the child's emotions. If the child cries, do not start rebuking the child or demanding that they stop crying. Rather, validate what the child is feeling. Say, "I know you are hurting so much; in your position, I would be crying too." A reply like this will make you look like a friend, you will not be the target for all the anger and anxiety the child feels. It is also likely that the child will open up to you more.

When you become a friend, the child will trust you because they feel that you are on their side, whether it is the right or wrong one. For example, if the child is angry at you and says that he or she does not want to see you and demands to be left alone, do so but assure the child that you love him or her and will be available if they want to talk. Let the child feel your support even in those tense moments.

Establishing trust also lets the child know that you trust their ability to process emotions properly, soaring his or her confidence.

Validation is also key to calming the child down. If you assure the child that you understand his or her feelings, it is unlikely that he or she shall respond in a defensive angry manner. When you acknowledge the child's feelings, his or her anger softens and the child is able to create room for learning how to cope and to empathize. If, on the other hand, you disregard these feelings, the child will fight to defend his or her sense of self.

Differentiate Emotion and Behavior

Kids do not know how to distinguish between anger and aggressive behavior. At least, from what has been modeled in real life and on TV, an angry person speaks violently, throws stuff around and will even hurt others. However, take the time and patiently teach your child how to label his or her feelings. Make the child verbalize them by using terms like disappointed, angry, irritated, frustrated and other like terms.

A child should understand that angry feelings are allowed, but aggressive behavior is wrong. You may say, "It is okay to be angry that your brother took the remote control, but it is not okay to yell at him." Help the child see that distinction. You will be surprised when the child comes to report to you when the brother takes the remote instead of crying or yelling. This is a positive response; ensure that you reward it.

Sometimes, the child will not be able to verbalize feelings only because he or she does not recognize them. To increase the child's knowledge of them, begin to talk about it and describe the feelings in simple language. Over time, the child will begin to describe these feelings better and this will enhance communication and understanding.

Exercise Patience

Patience is an incredibly valuable quality when dealing with children, one of the reasons being that you need to control yourself and the second being that you need to be more accommodating of their learning processes. One of the values many parents desire if you ask them is to be more patient with their children. They desire not to yell or curse when they have to repeat the same instructions time and again. They also desire to remain calm when their child is venting.

As an adult, you set the pace for how children in your household or under your care behave and to do this effectively, you may want to take some valuable steps. First, identify what triggers you to anger and take note of when and where this happens most times. For example, some people tend to lose their cool in the morning when they need to get to work or in the evening when they are tired or disappointed at what they find at home. Being in a hurry, tired, or disappointed will cause you to flare up fast at the slightest irritation. Once you have taken note of that, move on to work on your response.

Carefully observe what you do when prompted to anger. Observe how your body reacts. Does your heart beat faster, does it become difficult to breathe, or do your palms sweat? What thoughts creep up your mind as you listen to the child talk back? What response do you give? All these questions provide answers that will get you to understand your tipping point.

Just like when dealing with personal anger, come up with a plan of action that details what to do when the anger sets in. For example, you can use the time between getting from work to home to cool down and come up with an action plan of what you will do if you find that your expectations are not met. Also, plan on what to do in the heat of the moment like stepping away or breathing consciously to calm down. Plan also for what will follow once the emotions have cooled down. You could choose to sit by yourself to review the situation or sit with your child to discuss problem-solving methods.

With these steps, you will increasingly be calm in the face of provocation and be able to act rationally in front of your children. It will also give them the opportunity to learn and grow at their own pace without causing you multiple headaches.

Be Firm but Polite

Experts have taught on the need to be both kind and firm when dealing with children. Kindness shows the kid that you respect him or her as a person, while firmness shows the need to respect you. It also shows the seriousness of the situation. Both positive attributes are necessary to promote discipline and respect.

Many adults struggle with this truth fearing that they will become too permissive and accommodating of bad behavior. Others mistake kindness for pleasing the children or rushing to protect and rescue them from life's struggles and disappointments. However, kindness means respecting yourself and the child and validating each party's feelings. You are not kind when you condone disrespect from a child.

For example, if a child is yelling and hurling insults at you, the respectful thing to do is to walk out. This is quite controversial but you will see the reason behind it. Walking away is respecting yourself and not allowing the child to demean you. It actually sets a strong precedence for the child. Otherwise, you will engage in a yelling match or even find yourself becoming violent. Both of you have a better chance of calming down and discussing the matter later while in separate rooms. If you feel the need to take authority in this situation, send the kid to his room, which works too.

On the issue of firmness, the adult sets the rules, period. Adults are also responsible for enforcing them with lectures, boundaries, and punishments. However, this often invites power struggles. Therefore, instead of making it a solo activity, invite your kids to the table and discuss rules pertaining to anger management, among others. Talk about the rules, reasons for having rules, and each party's responsibility in keeping them.

To end, firmness and kindness create an environment of mutual understanding where everyone knows that they are valued and respected and that there is bound to be consequences if they do not reciprocate.

Take Extra Effort to Explain Their Emotions to Them

Children have a right to knowledge, especially concerning that which directly affects them and their feelings. They need to know that every feeling has an origin and that while some originate from good things, others like anger do not originate from good things. Explain to them that when anger comes about, it comes on as a strong feeling that seeks to take complete control but if you are cautious and diligent, you can control the extent to which it flares up.

Explain to them also that everyone experiences anger and that it is part of our natural feelings. Tell the child that anger comes because of fear, disappointment, hurt, loss, unfair treatment, and other negative things that all people suffer. Also demonstrate that when a person is angry, jaws feel tight, feet get cold or hot, muscles tighten, your stomach feels sick, you cry, scream, and may even feel like hurting others or themselves.

Teach the child how people look like when they are angry. Their faces look red, they become clumsy and walk fast, they bang things, their eyes water, the nose and mouth become pale, and the nostrils get wider. Explain any other signs that your child would recognize. Teach the child that anger can also be good if channeled into productive activities and give them ideas on what to do when angry instead of engaging in destructive things

It is said that information is power. With this knowledge, the child will be able to recognize when he, you, and other people are angry, and behave appropriately.

Acknowledge the Triggers and Drivers to Anger

Keenly observe the child to take note of situations, events, and circumstances that infuriate the child. At this stage, many things will irritate a child, but soon, a trend will emerge. Help the child avoid these triggers to get a handle of the situation and if avoiding them proves impossible, let your child understand them. Knowledge will help the child calm down.

If the child is grown and can monitor his emotions, he can manage them as well. Once the child understands the emotions that cause him to be angry, he can recognize them as they set in, take charge, and manage them before the emotions flare up.

Therapists recommend using art like painting, writing, and drawing to bring emotions to consciousness. These are excellent ways for children unable to recognize and verbalize their emotions to express what is disturbing them. Commend them for making an effort and encourage them to do it more often. It is also important to ask the child to explain the drawing, painting or writing, even when you can clearly see what it is. It helps teachers encourage them to verbalize emotions rather than relying on art all the time. This will make it easier for the child to develop a social life now and later in life.

Develop an Aggression Meter

Many families come up with rules that differentiate between acceptable and unacceptable behavior in expressing anger emotions. While some do not condone raising voices or slamming doors, others give room for such behavior. However, it is always better to avoid behavior like this to prepare your child to live with others in the future.

Setting clear standards means that while you may want to validate the child's feelings, ensure you do not make it seem like you are accepting of the bad behavior. Many of the rules of engagement set do not condone breaking stuff, showing disrespect, hitting others, and throwing things. In setting these rules, involve the children so that they are aware of the consequences of what they do. Children respond more positively to rules they help set.

The aggression meter should work for you too. Some parents lose it and get physical with their children. It could be a shove, a slap, a kick or an insult. Most times than not, the child retaliates and the fight escalates. While we may pretend that all of us are in control of their emotions, the truth is a number of us fail to do so sometimes. If you get caught in one of these, humble yourself and apologize. Say, "I apologize for losing control and shoving you." Only that. Do not start explaining to the child how his actions led you to do that, you want to teach responsibility and genuinely making amends, not excuses.

Adopt Negative Punishment (Time-Out) Instead of Positive Punishment

When a child breaks the anger rules in the house, it is only right if they receive punishment for their actions. Punishment is meant to decrease the probability of repeating undesired behavior and is often delivered immediately. Experts recommend negative punishment over positive punishment.

Negative punishment is that which happens when a desired item or incentive is taken away once the undesired behavior is presented. A child that enjoys swimming can be sent to detention as the rest take the swim class if they misbehave. A child that loves pancakes for breakfast can be forced to take something else for lashing out at his parent. If siblings start fighting over who gets to play a game first, the parent should take away the game altogether.

Positive punishment also presents a negative consequence for bad behavior but in a different way. A child who lashes out at his parents for not finding his favorite toy will be lectured on how to keep his toys properly. A child that breaks things when angry will be asked to collect the fragments as punishment. While both methods aim to lessen undesired behavior, the negative punishment strategy is clear about the negative consequences and reinforces the lesson better than the positive punishment method.

Be careful to punish behavior only, not anger. As long as the child is not breaking any rules, let him be. They too have a right to be angry. For example, if the child begins to swear at you in his outburst, make it clear that the consequence is meant to punish him for swearing. However, if all your child does is run to his room yelling how life is unfair, let it go. Give the child space and time he needs to blow off steam.

When you punish, do not be overly harsh. The way to do this is to refrain from punishing in the heat of your anger. If the child is screaming and yelling at you and you scream back punishments, the situation will only escalate. The child will keep going, and so will you. Here is where many parents lose control. However, if you take a moment, breath and ask yourself, "What lesson do I want my child to take from this?" The answer will give you a perspective on what you should do. It would be a sad affair if you joined your yelling child and yelled too. The secret to avoiding a chaotic home is to control your feelings while teaching your child to do the same.

Teach the Child Constructive Ways to Resolve Problems

Teach the child relaxation techniques like breathing and other self-calming tools that deflate anger and stress. This way, the child will take charge of his emotions even without needing help. These techniques not only work to lower agitation, but they also influence impulse control. The child may not get it or begin to practice immediately, but with encouragement and guidance, they will get better at it. For example, if you teach the child how to breathe in when he gets the urge to punch the wall, succeeding in this will make him gain a sense of control over what he feels and this lessens the possibility of acting out in other ways.

Model Proper Anger Expression

Heard of the expression 'Actions are louder than words'? Yes, children learn better from what the adults are modeling than from what is told to them. Even in your own life, you are likely to read into someone's character from what they do better than what they speak. We tend to exaggerate or give a false report in our speech but the real character comes out in the way we act. Therefore, if you as a parent becomes aggressive when overcome with anger, your child is likely to pick up that trait too. You will be teaching them that it is okay to hit others, yell, and become mean at the slightest provocation.

I bet you would prefer that your child dealt with anger appropriately. You want the child to learn how to regulate emotions, internalize their actions and thoughts, address the anger source, and think about how the child's reaction affects the situation and other people.

Although it is best to shield a child from adult issues, grab an opportunity to demonstrate a healthy way to deal with anger and frustration. It does not only demonstrate appropriate behavior; the kid gets to see that adults can be angry also. For example, if someone in your household leaves a tap running, say "I am angry that this person left the water running, but I will close the tap so that the water bill does not get so big." In saying this, the child will learn how to keep emotions in check and to take action.

In the event you are caught off guard and your child heard you yell or sees you behave irrationally, apologize for it. Tell the child that you are sorry and that you should have done better. Say "I am deeply sorry that you got to hear me yell when I was angry today. I was wrong to react that way. I should have gone to take a walk instead of raising my voice." With this statement, you get to correct your child's perception of the situation. However, do not repeatedly be caught doing the same thing, your apology will achieve the opposite result. The child will learn that it is okay to behave irrationally so long as you can give an apology to cover it all up later.

Avoid Subjecting the Child to Violent Influences

The least influence an angry child needs is which is brought by a violent atmosphere. Some parents believe that their children are unaffected by their angry outbursts, but the truth is children emulate everything they see. They read into the emotional atmosphere in the family to determine how safe they are. If the child perceives that the environment is not accommodating, he develops chronic anxiety or stress and at the slightest provocation, the child will fly off the handle just like his parents do.

Since a child's mind is still being shaped, a violent movie or video game causes them to think aggressive thoughts. You are able to distinguish between fiction and reality in a movie, though this ability slips from us sometime. However, a child will perceive that that's the way the world works. Keep off aggressive video games and movies, and ensure that the child has no access to them also.

Songs promoting violence or becoming friends with bullies also have the same effect because they program a child's mind thereby making him prone to aggression.

Family Member

The techniques you will need to deal with angry family members are similar to those you use to deal with your own anger, your partner's anger, and that of an angry child. If you have already mastered those ones, applying the knowledge to this situation will be easy. The techniques are:

- Control yourself.
- Be patient and respectful.
- Be firm and polite.
- Determine what triggers their anger.
- Show compassion and care.
- Indicate your desire to help them work through their emotions.

Chapter 7: Facts About Anger

Having discussed anger in depth, you already know what anger is, can identify signs of anger, know the origin of anger, its triggers and how to control it and to help others do the same. However, this chapter seeks to provide a more comprehensive and ordered description of facts about anger.

Here are some facts you need to know about anger.

- *Anger is not a bad emotion.*

    The belief that anger is bad is misconceived. In fact, anger is a natural emotion or response to an unsafe or uncharacteristic situation. There is nothing bad or good about a response, it is just a response. It is the driver that makes people confront unfairness and injustice. Just as hunger prompts you to eat, hunger prompts you to take action over an unfair situation.

- *Anger is not aggression.*

    Although anger and aggression are born of the same circumstances, they are quite different. Anger is the emotion or the frustration a person gets when expectations are not met. Aggression is the behavior by negative emotion that causes a person to want to destroy something or hurt someone such as by hitting, shoving, or slapping him/her. Foul language and name-calling are also part of the aggressive behavior. In essence, anger is the emotion that drives aggression.

- *Anger can motivate.*

We have established that anger causes a person to want to respond to an unfair situation or treatment. This response comes because anger causes a surge in energy that causes a person to feel indomitable. Although it is difficult to know what to do at the moment, the residual emotion can drive you to come up with a solution to a problem.

- *It is often a surface emotion.*

If you make an inquiry on what caused someone to act up when angry, you are likely to hear many responses starting with "I do not know what came over me…" This is not to mean that some alien being took control over the person, it means that they were not reacting to the unfair or rude treatment. Anger is more complicated than that. It originates from memories of pain and trauma experienced in the past which causes someone to become quite irritable at the slightest trigger. However, present factors like hunger, extreme thirst, pain, and extreme weather can put you on edge.

- *Anger indicates coping ability.*

Anger causes frustration and irritation that you may not even have to express in aggression. As different aggravating situations come along, you get to see how much of it you can bear. However, in the event you realize that you are not able to cope with a certain level of irritation in your life, you may seek for ways to help overcome that, including going for therapy. The secret to coping, however, is not in suppressing anger, but your ability to channel its energy to other productive ventures.

- *Anger affects your physiology.*

You may have noted changes in your body physiology when you became angry. Some people's heartbeat increases, muscles tense up, palms sweat while others start feeling their stomachs ache. Anger causes the release of adrenaline in the body, to charge you to either fight or fly. You are advised to express anger because when you do not, it feeds off itself affecting your physiology and the nervous system.

- *Anger causes life-threatening diseases and conditions.*

Chronic anger eats you off in the form of illnesses. When you are unable to overcome some form of pain and in return, it brings back bouts of anger, you can become physically ill or suffer conditions like heart attack and stroke. An unhealthy diet, smoking, failure to exercise, and other negative coping methods aggravate the effects of anger thereby increasing a person's susceptibility to serious heart conditions and diseases.

- *Anger is predictable.*

In an unpleasant or unfair situation, you would expect that a person would feel bad and become angry. The person will even be more upset if the unfair situation can be avoided and is only done by choice. This is the reason kids can predict how much their parents can be angry if they do something against the rules. Deception heightens anger levels.

- *Uncontrolled anger initiates problems.*

We associate anger with negative things because we understand that it can cause problems for people. Majority of those serving time in prison acted on anger and hurt others or damaged property. Anger also causes physical fights, arguments, damages relationships, and causes accidents that maim or kill. Some angry people result in substance use and abuse that cause health problems and death in the end. Uncontrolled anger is one of society's most dangerous poisons.

- *A person does not necessarily trigger anger.*

People are not the default sources of anger. The environment too can be a source of frustration and stress. For example, noise pollution for people living near airports, construction zones, train stations, and busy highways can trigger extreme anger even without them knowing. If you feel anger and cannot trace its source, how about listening to your environment to determine what could be annoying to you.

- *Humor beats anger.*

However angry you are, try laughing and voila! You will be on your high spirits again. Ever noticed how a funny comment lets your guard down during an argument? That is the beauty of laughter; it diffuses negative emotions and gets you smiling again. Although your concerns will continue to exist, you will be able to address them when calmer.

- *Relaxation reduces anger.*

Exercise, a good diet, and relaxation are the key antidotes for beating anger. If you are in a happy and relaxed mood, it is likely that a screaming child or a negative comment will just pass you by. You will barely notice it.

- *Blowing off steam is a bad idea.*

While punching a pillow is more socially acceptable than punching a face when angry, it may not do you good in the long run. It is obviously better to spare others from the effects of your anger by withdrawing to cool off, but this can intensify your anger issues. You develop aggression and are not able to exercise the ability to control yourself.

- *Anger is a gender thing.*

Although I would want to keep myself from discussing gender in this issue, it does play a role in how we express anger in society. In the West, and possibly across the globe also, anger is considered a masculine thing. Each gender is taught differently in regards to anger management. Girls are required to be passive while boys are encouraged to be aggressively angry. Adult men are likely to express anger physically by punching something while women find it hard to express it but with tears. As a result, women keep anger longer than men do. However, neither of the sexes has adopted a good coping method.

Chapter 8: Anger Management Goals

Anger management is good for a number of reasons. It helps people identify their stressors, monitor their reaction to it, let out the anger in a positive manner, and identify the origin of this vicious cycle. People are taught how to stay calm in heated environments, how to respond to angry people, and when to walk out of the situation.

However, the ultimate anger management goal is simple. It is to help a person reduce his anger. Anger is reduced when you are able to take charge of the physical and emotional stimulation it causes. It is impossible to avoid all situations and persons that can provoke you to anger but you can learn to respond to these people and situations in a cool manner.

One of the most popular misconceptions is that anger management is meant to give you anger suppression skills, but this is not the case. In fact, preventing anger is not a feasible goal. Anger is a normal emotion and you will experience it regardless of the effort you make to avoid it. Anger management skills and therapy only come in to try to unmask the reason behind the intense negative emotions and to express them in a healthy way. When you manage anger in this manner, you will not only feel lighter, but your past unmet needs, hurts, and pains will be addressed. You become a champion at addressing issues in your life and helping others address issues affecting them.

Learning anger management skills takes time and a lot of self-evaluation work, but the more you do it, the easier it gets. The payoffs also make it worth trying, at least. You build better relationships, repair broken ones, maintain your health, and live a more satisfying life.

Anger Management Therapy

Some people find it rather difficult to get to the core of their anger issues and will need professional help doing that. Others have difficulty practicing relaxation techniques while others are unable to channel the energy they get from anger to a healthy cause. Sometimes you may assume that you finally have a grip of it and your confidence crumbles down on your next outburst. This is where a therapist steps in.

When going through anger management therapy, a client receives guidance and training on a number of recovery guidelines. Clients get to have a platform on which they can release their emotions safely and in a controlled manner. In therapy, the expression is guided by questions. With these questions, the therapist primarily seeks to extract productive responses from the client.

The primary advantage of taking therapy rather than doing the anger management process on your own is that therapy gets deeper to the problems underlying. Clients still get to examine their anger triggers, analyze the emotions they feel in each stage of arousal, and learn to look out for the signs that precede anger. It is also typical of angry people to be in denial, which means that managing anger by themselves may not be as productive as it would be guided by a professional. Therapists are also able to analyze the body's response to past, current, and future events by examining their emotional reaction to specific stimuli. This process is meant to identify the body's defense mechanisms that could impede treatment.

An important thing to take note is that anger management is not only designed to help the victims, but it also helps the people surrounding them. For example, if you have an angry spouse or an angry child, you can take up therapy to learn how to handle them properly. Exposure to uncontrollable anger may lead to serious psychological, physiological, and physical problems for you. However, therapy will help you manage your response to an angry outburst and equip you with skills to help your loved one calm down.

Clients taking anger management therapy have the option of taking their classes individually or in a group setting. Individual therapy involves the client working with the professional one-on-one. It is particularly suitable for clients with privacy issues such as those who may not be comfortable talking about deep sensitive issues to a group of people. Other clients choose it for its convenience to their schedules. Meanwhile, group therapy calls for clients to go through treatment as a team. A class is designed to address a particular issue, which means that persons in each class have experienced the same problem and are able to relate and empathize with each other. Examples of classes include the work-related anger class, teen class, relationship issues class, and the teen class.

The classes are available continually at the treatment centers or as an online course. Therapists give home exercises and assignments because these are thought to make the process more efficient. People in therapy are also encouraged to practice the skills they learn in their day-to-day life. Therapy, therefore, allows the clients to learn and practice concurrently, which improves their understanding and the ability to control anger. In addition, if a technique is not working, the therapist can dig up another based on his experience in the practice.

Professional services are also superior to personal home treatment because anger is often tied to other serious mental health problems. It is likely that a therapist will diagnose these problems in the course of treating anger. These conditions include a narcissistic personality, depression, bipolar disorder, posttraumatic stress disorder (PTSD), and oppositional defiant disorder (ODD). These conditions cause a person to have uncontrollable anger outbursts at the least provocation. Children that are exhibiting extreme hostility and anger could be suffering from ODD. If basic control strategies are not working, it is best to try professional help because it might result in a diagnosis, which is a step towards treatment.

Professional help is also important because chronic anger leads to behavioral problems. People who suffer from constant eruptions of anger are more likely to take on substance abuse, which typically starts at an early age. Teens who abuse drugs rarely complete or further their education. The use of drugs also significantly ruins a user's ability to control their impulses. These people, therefore, need urgent intervention in the form of therapy.

A therapist is devoted to helping her clients acquire skills to manage their overpowering emotions. The services may also help to address underlying pain and memories that could be the root of the distress. With patience and persistence, it is possible to control any anger level.

Persons Who Can Benefit

Our judicial system is at liberty to mandate persons sued for aggression and anger-related issues to attend court-ordered anger management class to help them regain control of their anger. Typically, these people have committed criminal offenses, but offenses like battery and assault, destruction of property, disturbance of the peace, and violence against an intimate partner also get people taking these mandatory classes.

Persons working in the health care and business fields are advised to take anger management classes to avoid the risk of becoming irritated and frustrated while handling customers. People seeking to improve the nature of their relationships with their children, friends, and family members are also suitable candidates for this class. Other social groups to whom this therapy is recommended include persons who use or are recovering from substance use and misuse, those suffering from traumatic brain injury, and persons with mental health problems. Violent criminals and bullies are also advised to seek professional help managing their anger.

Conclusion

Thanks for making it through to the end of *Anger Management: Ultimate Guide to Master Your Emotions, Identify, and Control Anger to Completely Take Back Your Life*, let's hope it was informative and able to provide you with all the tools you need to achieve your goals whatever they may be. Certainly, you were able to refresh your memory and learn new things about anger, detecting it, and resolving it for you and for those around you.

Anger is a healthy emotion that is common to all, but most people lose their temper at some point in their lives. Those who do not have outbursts today did have them at some point in life however blatant or subtle it may be, nevertheless, they learned to control and channel it properly. This should be a ray of hope because it shows that you, your partner, child, or family member can achieve the same through consistent practice.

The next step is to dip your feet right into the pool and begin to practice what you read therein. While you may have already mastered some of the steps indicated, whether pertaining to your anger issue or of those around you, feel free to start the process afresh. Starting the process all over again will not hurt, it will only make you an expert at what you are doing. You might also be lucky enough to notice new things you had not identified before. After all, our bodies and emotions evolve continually.

If you experience difficulty taking up the process of managing anger by yourself, know that it is important to seek professional help. Anger management therapists are trained to help you overcome anger in a controlled way and in a safe space. As discussed earlier, you will find that the therapy sessions are structured strategically to handle your issue in one-on-one sessions or in active interaction with like-minded people in a group session.

www.ingramcontent.com/pod-product-compliance
Lightning Source LLC
Chambersburg PA
CBHW031110080526
44587CB00011B/914